THE HISTORY OF THE PANZERWAFFE
VOLUME 3: THE PANZER DIVISION

THE HISTORY OF THE PANZERWAFFE

VOLUME 3: THE PANZER DIVISION

Thomas Anderson

OSPREY PUBLISHING
Bloomsbury Publishing Plc
PO Box 883, Oxford, OX1 9PL, UK
1385 Broadway, 5th Floor, New York, NY 10018, USA
E-mail: info@ospreypublishing.com
www.ospreypublishing.com

OSPREY is a trademark of Osprey Publishing Ltd

First published in Great Britain in 2020

ISBN: HB: 978 1 4728 3389 1
eBook: 978 1 4728 3388 4
ePDF: 978 1 4728 3390 7
XML: 978 1 4728 3391 4

20 21 22 23 24   10 9 8 7 6 5 4 3 2 1

Conceived and edited by Jasper Spencer-Smith
Design by Briony Hartley
Index by Shaun Barrington
Produced for Bloomsbury Publishing Plc by Editworks Limited,
Bournemouth BH1 4RT, UK
Originated by PDQ Digital Media Solutions, Bungay, UK
Printed and bound in India by Replika Press Private Ltd.

Osprey Publishing supports the Woodland Trust,
the UK's leading woodland conservation charity.

To find out more about our authors and books visit
www.ospreypublishing.com. Here you will find extracts, author
interviews, details of forthcoming events and
the option to sign up for our newsletter.

FSC
MIX
Paper from
responsible sources
FSC® C016779
www.fsc.org

CONTENTS

Introduction   6

1: Origins   20

2: The Elements of a Panzer Division   32

3: The Panzer Division   68

4: Rifle Brigade   102

5: Combat Elements   122

6: Ancillary Units   238

Index   283

Acknowledgements   288

INTRODUCTION

The British and French were the progenitors of what was at the time a revolutionary weapon: both nations deployed relatively large numbers of tanks to break the bloody stalemate of trench warfare. The British first sent their tanks into action for the Battle of Flers-Courcelette in September 1916: French tanks were first used in battle during 1917. The first time the tank was to have a significant effect on the battlefront was in November 1917, at the launch of the Battle of Cambrai, when British tanks smashed through enemy trench systems, allowing infantry to capture long-held territory. After the war, both nations continued to develop the tank to equip their armoured forces. Also British and French manufacturers began to export their products all over the world.

Many foreign nations procured licenses to manufacture various types for their armed forces, whereas other nations began the process of producing their own types designed to meet their specific requirements. Using expertise gained in World War I, the British and French began to offer training facilities for many of these burgeoning armoured forces.

In 1918, Germany was held solely responsible for the war by the Allied nations. In 1919, the Treaty of Versailles was signed and among the conditions negotiated was that Germany would not only pay vast sums in reparations, but was also forbidden to design, develop, manufacture or possess any heavy mobile weapons: Germany was a broken nation. Article 171 stated:

> Likewise, the production of armoured cars, tanks and any similar material, which can be used for war by Germany is strictly forbidden, as is their import into Germany.

Left:
The *Panzerkommandant* (tank commander) of a PzKpfw IV Ausf D of PzRgt 7 in 10.PzDiv; a silhouette of a charging Bison - the symbol of the regiment - has been stencilled on the side of the turret. Tanks such as the PzKpfw III and PzKpfw IV formed the backbone of the German *Panzerwaffe*.

Above:
Elements of 1.PzDiv, including infantry, prepare for battle during *Fall Rot* (Case Red) the second phase of the French campaign which was launched on 5 June 1940. On the horizon are elements of the tank force that include PzKpfw III and PzKpfw IV and a number of PzKpfw I and PzKpfw II light tanks.

German military officials and planners continuously attempted to find ways around the terms set out in the treaty, but in reality they would have to accept that the forces they commanded would only be large enough to defend their country. The Allied governments had achieved their most important objective.

In Germany, the treaty was commonly referred to as the '*Schandvertrag*,' (disgraceful treaty) and very, very few Germans accepted the reparations imposed: particularly those financial and in materials. This became the breeding ground for the unrest which made it easy for the nationalist parties to undermine the new, as yet untested, democracy. In particular, the *Nationalsozialistische Deutsche Arbeiterpartei* (NSDAP – National Socialist German Workers' Party) headed by Adolf Hitler, exploited the increasing

fervour of populism in reactionary circles, the unemployed and those disconnected from society; finally affecting ordinary people. Hitler came to power in 1933, after a somewhat questionable 'democratic' election, and began his quest to build an all-conquering Germany.

Many historians have concluded that the terms in the Treaty of Versailles were somewhat unbalanced, in parts unjust and politically extremely unwise. John Frederick Charles Fuller, the pioneer of armoured warfare, who although being closely acquainted with fascist movements in Europe and Great Britain, expressed his views in the following note:

> The Treaty of Versailles was signed by the Germans on 28 June 1919 in the most critical situation for the country... for this reason, it was morally null and void.

Right:
A *Panzerkompanie* (tank company), possibly from 1.PzDiv, assembles in open territory during the *Polenfeldzug* (Poland campaign) which was launched on 1 September 1940. All most every type of tank, motor vehicle, truck and even horse-drawn transport used by the unit are visible – a strange assemblage, but a truly independent and effective fighting force.

The *Reichsheer*

In the critical period after World War I, *Generaloberst* Johannes 'Hans' Friedrich Leopold von Seeckt became chief of staff in the *Reichswehr*, the successor of the German Imperial Army. By making best use of the limited resources available to him, he built a reorganized, reasonably equipped highly disciplined military force. Although there were constant changes in the government, von Seekt succeeded in maintaining stability in his military. He was sure that the small forces approved by the Allies were nothing more (and nothing less) than the core of a modern army, which would emerge at the appropriate time. The resulting *Reichsheer*, despite being limited in both size and equipment, became an elite army with a young, skilled and enthusiastic leadership.

In the 1920s, von Seeckt and his staff, supported by his enthusiastic young officers, began to work on the tactics to be deployed in any future armed conflict, thus laying the foundation of the later *Wehrmacht*. He of course had his own views; for him France and Poland were the prime opponents

of Germany on mainland Europe. But in 1926, von Seeckt retired from the military and was replaced by *Generaloberst* August Wilhelm Heye.

In 1927, von Seeckt published a document, *Ansichten zur modernen Kavallerie* (Views on Modern Cavalry), in which he asserted that the motor vehicle would be essential to the creation of a new, mobile unitary force able to transport men, guns and material – he subsequently attended and supported the extensive development trials of early tanks and aircraft held, in total secrecy, at Kama in the Soviet Union. Many German pilots and tank crews were trained at the facility in the years leading up to the war.

In the late 1920s, his ideas were taken up by two staff officers at a lower command level; Wilhelm Heye and Kurt von Hammerstein-Equord who refined them before they were sent to *Generalmajor* Oswald Lutz and, as he was then, *Oberstleutnant* Heinz Guderian to be implemented. It was around this time that motorized reconnaissance was transferred from the cavalry to the *Kraftfahrtruppen* (motorized forces), which must have been quite difficult for the proud horsemen to accept. In 1929, the *Kraftfahrtruppen*

Left:
Tanks and supporting vehicles of 2.PzDiv, during the retreat from Bryansk in the summer of 1943, are vulnerable to air attack as they cross open countryside. Simplifying the design of armoured personnel carriers and self-propelled artillery pieces allowed a greater number of each type to be delivered to the Panzer divisions. Although PzKpfw VI Tiger tanks are visible, the type was only ever deployed at army group level.

Above:
A column of the rifle regiment of 1.PzDiv: Several SdKfz 251, armoured half-track vehicles, are being used to tow the le FH 18 field howitzer. Unfortunately, such a column would be followed by a very conspicuous cloud of dust.

were reorganized and elevated to the same level as the infantry and cavalry. The responsible office was *Inspektion 6 (In 6)*, which was led by *Generalleutnant* Otto von Stülpnagel, who was to become *Inspekteur der Kraftfahrtruppen*, and directly superior to Lutz and Guderian.

The many new ideas were bitterly opposed by many of the older officers serving with the infantry or the cavalry. Even von Stülpnagel was not convinced that the ideas promoted by Lutz and Guderian regarding the possible value of the tank forces were acceptable.

When Stülpnagel retired in March 1931, he sent a note to Guderian:

Believe me; neither of us will live to see German tanks running.

1931 to 1934

In the early 1930s, *Generalmajor* Lutz, Chief of Staff of In 6, began to seek out young and capable officers to join motorized troops; well-known names

like Walther Nehring and Werner Kempf were among those selected.

At the same time, Insp 6 began to work out the organizational structures, which at the time were no more than ideas on paper, for important sections of the future motorized army: The *Panzertruppe* (armoured forces), the *Aufklärungstruppe* (motorized reconnaissance forces) and finally the *Panzerabwehrtruppe* (anti-tank defence forces).

The first motorized 'armoured' units were rapidly established, but this forced the personnel to be trained using mock wooden tanks, built over light cars or even bicycles. Guderian was responsible for implementing the training programme for what were to become the all-conquering Panzer divisions. He had concluded that the tank was a versatile weapon and had his own vision as to how the type would be deployed in battle. He was adamant that the Panzer force would not be used as cavalry, as it was with Great Britain, France and the Soviet Union, to support an infantry assault, since he felt that the type could be used in a number of roles, but mainly to break through enemy's

Above:
Concentrating tanks and other vehicles in a small area was a dangerous practice, being open to attack by patrolling enemy aircraft or long-range artillery. The tanks, PzKpfw 38(t) and PzKpfw IV, are from 7.PzDiv which was under the command of Erwin Rommel.

front-line positions. But he was also aware that as a ground war unfolded then more advanced tanks would have to be designed and developed.

Guderian realized that to use the tank to its full potential it would need to be supported by a dedicated organizational structure. At this point it should be noted that he was not the first to have such thoughts: Colonel Charles de Gaulle, who commanded the 4e *Division Cuirassée* (4e DCr – 4th Armoured Division), had a similar vision for a tank deployment.

Ultimately, Guderian saw a requirement for a new type of highly specialized unit organized as self-contained force – almost a small army – to propagate offensive rather than defensive warfare: in essence a Panzer division.

Obviously a Panzer division would be equipped with tanks, but would also contain many other supporting units, including a significant number of reconnaissance and signals units, integrated artillery, anti-tank and anti-aircraft units, and also contain bridge-layer units. The division would also have a dedicated workshop and engineers, medical facilities and even a bakery.

A series of manoeuvres was carried out before 1939 to practise deployment and operational (tactical) methods, over various types of terrain and in all weather conditions, to perfect the fighting prowess of the division.

But in 1932, much of the required equipment and manpower to implement this far-reaching programme was not available; the high command of the military and the general staff lacked interest, there was a serious shortage of suitable equipment, and Germany remained constricted by severe financial conditions.

Left:
A camera team from the propaganda company with their camera mounted on the engine cover of a PzKpfw IV from 7.PzDiv. Film units covered field manoeuvres and action on the battlefront to be shown as newsreels to bolster public morale.

Below:
The *Aufklärung-Abteilung* (reconnaissance battalion) (mot) in a Panzer division was issued with four- and eight-wheeled reconnaissance and radio cars. This establishment proved to be effective, although the 2cm-armed SdKfz 222 and SdKfz 231 or SdKfz 232 were the preferred vehicles of reconnaissance units.

Left:
In the years leading up to World War II, the German military held a number of vast displays to demonstrate the growth and fighting capabilities of newly developed weaponry. In this image, taken from a propaganda film, PzKpfw I tanks burst through a smoke screen to launch an attack on 'enemy' positions.
(SZ Photo)

CHAPTER 1

ORIGINS

In 1932, *Inspektur* 6 organized an exercise for motorized reconnaissance forces which was to take place in Silesia; the objective was to evaluate the effectiveness (mobility) of reconnaissance units on the battlefront. The final report on the exercise concluded that an infantry (foot) reconnaissance unit could march at 4kph, a horse-mounted (cavalry) unit could travel at 6kph to 8kph, while a motorized reconnaissance unit could achieve over 20kph. The proponents for motorizing the military were most encouraged, as they felt this would open the way to the formation of an all-powerful mechanized force.

In 1933, Guderian was faced with a fresh problem; Adolf Hitler was elected *Reichskanzler* (Chancellor) and a large number of officers and officials from the more conservative circles in the military rushed to support their 'new' Führer. For Guderian it was no surprise to find that the majority – mainly elderly officers – in the *Generalstab des Heeres* (GenStbdH – General Staff of the Army), rejected his revolutionary plans. One in particular, *Generaloberst* Ludwig Beck, who became head of the *Truppenamt* (a high-level department attached to the GenStbdH) in October 1933 – two years later he became the Chief of the General Staff – vehemently opposed any proposal made by Guderian in regard to large armoured formations.

By early 1934, all opposition had collapsed and almost immediately the decision was taken to establish three Panzer divisions with a further three to follow: The beginning of the *Panzerwaffe*.

In 1933, *Panzerschule* (tank training school) Kama in the Soviet Union was closed and all the personnel and equipment were redeployed to establish

Above:
The *Panzerspähwagen* (*sechtsrad* [6 Rad] – six wheeled) was the first heavy armoured car to enter service with German reconnaissance units, but since the type used a lengthened chassis and the running gear of a commercial truck it lacked cross-country mobility. However, the bullet-deflecting shape of the superstructure was adopted for later German heavy armoured cars. The version shown was designated SdKfz 232 (Fu) and fitted with long-range radio equipment, as indicated by the frame-type antenna.

the *Kraftfahr-Lehr-Kommando* (vehicle training command), a secret unit based at Zossen some 30km south of Berlin. This was also the site of the underground headquarters for the *Oberkommando der Wehrmacht* (OKW – High Command of German Armed Forces) and the *Oberkommando des Heeres* (OKH – High Command of the Army). A second base was established at *Truppenübungsplatz* (troop training grounds), Ohrdruf in Thuringa.

However, there was a shortfall in the number of personnel to be trained and as an expedient men were transferred from disbanded horse-cavalry units; a clever move, as it gave the highly disciplined troopers from this old and proud branch of the army a new and exciting future.

Equipment

Military planners now began the task of procuring the most effective equipment for the new *Panzerwaffe*, but there would many problems to overcome. When German officials were once again invited to observe military exercises in various countries they were not only able to examine the latest fighting vehicles, but also how each nation would use them in battle. Great Britain, France and the Soviet Union had built up large armoured formations by the beginning of the 1930s. Much of this equipment used World War I technology, but there would always be a number of 'modern' types on display. The above nations and the USA placed a great emphasis on heavy armour rather than on speed and mobility, but around 1937/38 this changed in favour of the faster, more agile cavalry (cruiser) tank. Most of these were armed with a 37mm or 40mm gun, but a number mounted a 75mm gun for support duties.

The Soviet Union during the same period introduced a vast number of armoured vehicles into service, focusing mainly on two types; the T-26, a light infantry tank with conventional running gear, and the BT series of fast cavalry tanks fitted with Christie-type suspension. Both types mounted a 45mm gun.

Influenced by these observations, Lutz and Guderian made contingency plans to introduce two types of tank into service. One, designated the *Zugführerwagen* (ZW – platoon commander vehicle [later PzKpfw III]), was armed with a 3.7cm tank gun and would become the main battle tank: the other designated *Panzerbefelswagen* (BW – armoured command vehicle [later PzKpfw IV]), armed with a 7.5cm gun, was to provide support fire using high-explosive (HE) ammunition. In line with current operational

Below:
Any enemy tank which had been captured intact, such as this Soviet BT-7, would be used by German armoured forces. They were most commonly used by *Feldpolizei-Einheiten* (field police units) or for training purposes.

Above:

A *Maschinengewehr-Kraftwagen* (Kfz 13), which entered service with armoured car companies in 1933, was built on a strengthened passenger car chassis and armed with an MG 13. The vehicle follows an SdKfz 232 (6 Rad), armed with a 2cm cannon and an MG 13, across a pontoon bridge during an exercise in the mid-1930s.

thinking, mobility was considered to be more important than armour protection.

It was anticipated that the ZW and BW tanks would enter service in 1937 and equip the first Panzer divisions being established.

In the late 1920s, Krupp had worked with Landswerk in Sweden on the design of tracked vehicles and used the experience gained to develop the *Landwirtschaftlicher-Akerschlepper* (LaS – agricultural tractor). The prototype tanks utilized the Krupp-built chassis and were fitted with a light-armour superstructure manufactured by Daimler-Benz. The type, armed with two *Maschinengewehr* (MG – machine gun) 13, was subsequently designated the *Panzerkampfwagen* (PzKpfw – tank) I. In 1934, Henschel received a contract to produce 150 of the type.

The production of the LaS was an important step for the German armaments industry which, until then, had little or no experience of the engineering required to mass manufacture tanks. It would become a steep learning process for those companies involved.

Production PzKpfw I tanks were to be delivered to the training units for the newly forming Panzer divisions, but production was slow, resulting in a lack of complete vehicles. Training units were forced to use the basic chassis, without armoured superstructure, as driving instruction vehicles.

In 1936, it was acknowledged that the planned delivery dates for the ZW [PzKpfw III] and BW [PzKpfw IV] would not be achieved, and planners decided to increase production of the PzKpfw I. The new version mounted a 2cm light canon and was designated LaS-100 [later PzKpfw II].

For crew training, the lack of ZW and BW tanks was overcome by using a simple solution: the turret on an available PzKpfw I or PzKpfw II was painted with a geometric pattern to disguise it as the larger type.

Below:
The *Begleitwagen* (BW – escort tank) was originally intended to support the tank assault. Later designated PzKpfw IV, the type would become the most important weapon of the Panzer division. This is an Ausf A; the first production version.

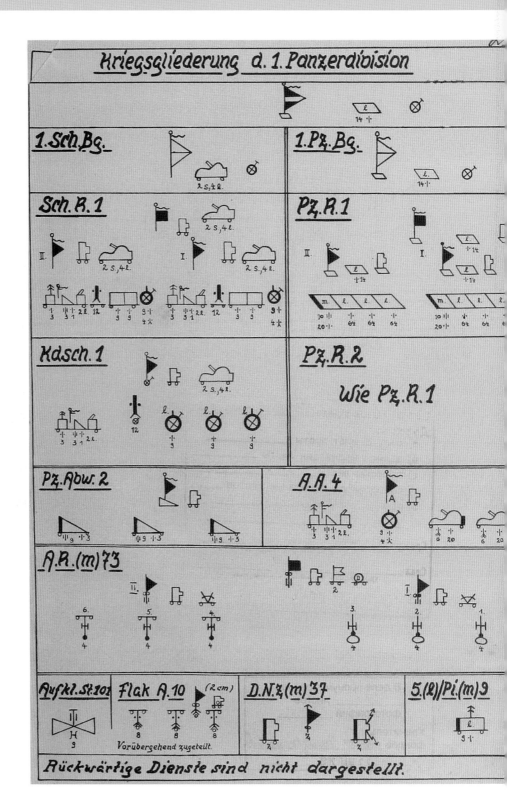

Right:
The basic structure for 1.PzDiv which was published before the first series of exercises in August 1935: Note the important supply units are not shown.

Organization

The revolutionary thinking by the creators of the *Panzerwaffe* also required some unorthodox solutions for the organizational structure of the force. A Panzer division was intended to be an autonomous unit capable of launching a spearhead offensive operation, break through the enemy frontline and continue to advance. Following forces would spread out and attack the enemy on the flanks before advancing on his rear positions to capture supply and communications echelons. Secondary units would then perform a mopping-up operation to clear any remaining enemy troops from the battlefront.

To enable a Panzer division to effectively achieve its objective required a number of highly effective specialized subunits to be integrated within the force.

Above:
During the period of establishment, the first Panzer divisions had to utilize old or obsolete equipment. In the foreground is a PzKpfw I armed with two *Maschinengewehr* (MG – machine gun) 13 and behind it is a 10.5cm *leichter Feldhaubitz* (le FH – light field howitzer) 16 which was issued in World War I.

Structure

To be effective in battle, ideally each Panzer division would be formed as follows:

Divisional staff
Panzer brigade
Infantry brigade
Anti-tank defence battalion
Reconnaissance battalion
Artillery regiment
Signals battalion
Pioneer elements
Transport, supply, workshop, medical and other services

At the embryonic phase, great uncertainty surrounded the formation of the Panzer divisions and the size of each element could vary considerably. After the first trials, under simulated battle conditions in the late 1930s, sufficient experience and information had been gained to influence the final organizational structure of a Panzer division.

The Divisional Staff Section was the command echelon for the Panzer division and was formed as follows; a staff company, a motorcycle company and light tank company.

The Tank Force: A Panzer brigade consisted of two Panzer regiments with two Panzer battalions each having a heavy company and three light tank companies.

Right:
The PzKpfw II, armed with a 2cm KwK 30 and an MG 34, was intended to supplement German armoured forces until sufficient numbers of the PzKpfw III and PzKpfw IV were being produced to equip the new Panzer divisions.

The Infantry Element had a *Schützen* (rifle) regiment and a *Kradschützen* (motor-cycle mounted battalion).

An Infantry Brigade comprised one *Schützen* regiment with two *Schützen* battalions and a *Kradschützen* battalion

The Anti-tank Element (3.7cm PaK) consisted of a battalion of three companies each equipped with nine guns.

The Reconnaissance Battalion comprised two reconnaissance companies, a motorcycle company and a heavy company. Initial reconnaissance would have been provided by the *Luftwaffe*.

The Divisional Artillery Regiment at that time was only equipped with the 10.5cm *leichter Feldhaubitz* (leFH – light field howitzer) 18. (It is interesting to note that one battalion was equipped with self-propelled guns. This Motorized Artillery Regiment consisted of the following; one towed battalion of three batteries, each with four 10.5cm leFh 18; a self-propelled battalion of three batteries, each with four self-propelled 10.5cm leFh 18).

The Signals Battalion comprised two companies and supplied communications for the divisional staff.

Workshop services were provided by an engineer company.

The strength, organization and level of equipment in these subunits was the subject of continual change.

Above:
British forces abandoned large numbers of serviceable vehicles in the aftermath of the Dunkirk evacuation. When France surrendered, vast numbers of motor cars and trucks (also manufacturers) became available to German forces. Here an anti-tank company has been equipped with ex-British army Morris Commercial CS 8 to tow a 3.7cm PaK.

Left:
German pioneers have
filled a defensive anti-tank
ditch, dug by British and
Commonwealth forces, to
allow a PzKpfw IV to cross
and continue in pursuit
of the retreating enemy.
(SZ Photo)

CHAPTER 2

THE ELEMENTS OF A PANZER DIVISION

German military planners, in general, lacked experience when it came to selecting equipment and even less when it came to organizational matters. This lack of perspective led to disagreements which in turn became – occasionally personal – long-running disputes. Many of these were to last throughout the war and become the cause of frequent changes to the organizational tables, and also complicate future developments.

The economic situation, lack of vital materials and poor production performance in the Reich exacerbated matters. From 1940, no Panzer division would ever be similarly equipped and never to the standard published in *Kriegstärkenachweisung* (KStN – table of organization).

As World War II progressed this inconsistency became accepted as the norm.

However, a number of important changes were influenced by experience gained from combat. After the victorious campaigns in Poland and France, the *Organisations-Abteilung* (OrgAbt – organization department) issued questionnaires to a number of units which then were ordered to supply accurate after-action reports. These were then carefully evaluated by staff which led to the OrgAbt suggesting several changes to a number of parts in the organization of armoured forces.

Adolf Hitler had thought that *Unternehmen* (Operation) Barbarossa, the invasion of Russia, would be completed in a few weeks, but it became an epic struggle and as the Russian winter arrived German forces faced the nightmare of defeat. Due to the conditions on the battlefront, after-action reports were sent to the OrgAbt at a slower pace for evaluation which, in turn, delayed implementation.

Left:
A column of vehicles from AufklAbt 3 (mot) in 3.PzDiv crosses over a temporary bridge on the River Marne during the advance into France. The lead vehicle is a Guy Ant, one of the vast numbers of vehicles abandoned by British forces as they retreated from France. The vehicle is followed by an SdKfz 222, the mainstay of German armoured reconnaissance units.

Above:
The Volkswagen (VW) *Typ 82 Kübelwagen* (bucket car). The type was designed as a light passenger-carrying vehicle as part of the vehicle standardization programme initiated by German military planners.

Far right:
The *Typ* 82 used the chassis of the Porsche-designed '*Kraft durch Freude-Wagen*' (KDF-W – 'power through joy car') (later VW Beetle). A 25hp air-cooled four-cylinder engine and the transmission was mounted at the rear.

The first major occurrence which delayed the establishment of the Panzer divisions was the conversion of the light mechanized divisions (1.leDiv, 2.leDiv, 3.leDiv and 4.leDiv) to full-sized Panzer divisions. But due to a shortage of equipment, only 1.leDiv received the number of tanks considered adequate to form a division.

In late 1940, two decisions were made which would result in further fundamental changes to the Panzer divisions. Firstly, the PzKpfw I light tank was thought to be obsolete and inadequate for the battlefield and increasing numbers were withdrawn from active service. Secondly, the PzKpfw II was only to be used to equip *leichte Panzer-Zug* (light tank platoons) deployed for reconnaissance duties. Importantly, all redundant divisions were to be re-equipped to form the new Panzer divisions. Put simply, the number of tank divisions was doubled by reducing the number of tanks in each division by 50 per cent. As an example, in 1.PzDiv the total number of tanks was almost halved – during the Polish campaign the division had some 300 tanks, but for the invasion of France this number was reduced to 256; a year later only 145 were available.

Above:
The motorcycle was a very cost-effective way to rapidly deploy a significant infantry force. The BMW R11 *Beiwagen-Krad* (motorcycle and sidecar combination), which carried a crew of three, was one of the types chosen to equip the *Kradschützen* (motorcycle infantry). The lead combination mounts a *Maschinengewehr* (MG – machine gun) 13.

[Note: The above provides an outline of a 'typical' tank division, the subunits and also support services. This has been achieved by examining standard KStN organizational tables and other wartime documents found in military archives.]

Organization

German units were established with equipment (vehicles and weapons) according to KStN which were prepared and published by the organizational department of the *Generalstab des Heeres* (GenStbdH – General Staff of the Army).

However, the supply of designated equipment did not always exactly follow the numbers published in the structures. From the time Great Britain declared war on Germany, the build-up of German forces would be

plagued by financial and production problems. One solution was to supply units with non-standard equipment which over time became more or less standard practice.

When a new KStN was published, it was usual practice to destroy the previous edition. Due to this fact many early KStN have disappeared, and those stored in the *Heeresarchiv* (army archive) in Potsdam were destroyed by Allied bombing in 1945.

Procurement

In the mid-1930s, when the *Wehrmacht* was at the stage of being established, there was a complicated procedure to be followed for the procurement of motor vehicles. For those responsible at all levels, the question of motorization and the distribution of vehicles would be the cause of a

Above:
The markings stencilled on in front of the spare wheel indicate that this *Kübelwagen* is in service with a *Generalkommando* (army corps). Although lacking four-wheel drive, the lightweight (750kg) vehicle was fitted with a ZF self-locking differential which allowed it to be driven over the sands of North Africa and through the deep mud in Northern Russia.

Left:
The French-built Laffly W 15 T had all-wheel-drive and was supplied to the army as an artillery tractor for towing the 155mm Canon de 155 model 1877/14 Scheinder. The auxiliary wheels fitted at the front, were positioned to assist with ditch crossing. After France capitulated, production continued and the type was supplied to *Wehrmacht* units. By 1944, some 1,300 vehicles had been built. Here a Ford Eifel staff car is being recovered from a river.

number of problems. However, it became obvious to those involved that the formation of Panzer divisions required preferential treatment.

Soft-skinned vehicles

To provide troops with mobility, the motorcycle (also bicycle) was a simple choice for the newly established *Wehrmacht*. Being relatively simple and cheap to produce, the many German motorcycle manufacturers were already involved in mass producing them for the public and also export. A vast number of types were readily available: light (up to 350cc), medium (350 to 500cc) and heavy (over 500cc). The medium and heavy motorcycles could be fitted with a sidecar – known as a combination.

A number of civilian-type passenger cars were also an important part of the motorization programme. In the late 1920s, standard production commercial trucks began to be procured and would be identified in official documents by an 'o' prefix. In the 1930s, design and development began for the production of specialized military vehicles; many of the proposed types were expected to have excellent cross-country performance.

The German military introduced a classification system, but the exact date of application is unknown. The term *Sonderkraftfahrzeug* (SdKfz – special purpose motor vehicle) was introduced for combat vehicles;

Below:
The Adler *Typ* 10N, built on the chassis of the Standard 6 saloon car, was known as the *Kübelsitzwagen* (bucket seat car). The type was fitted with simple open bodywork and fitted with military-pattern rough terrain tyres. Note the fascine (a bundle of tree branches) ready to be used if the vehicle becomes bogged down.

other vehicles were designated *Kraftfahrzeug* (Kfz – motor vehicle). Trailers were designated in a similar way, all types used for military purposes were known as *Sonderanhänger* (SdAnh – special purpose trailer or *Anhänger* (Anh – trailer).

Two manuals describing this system were published; D 601+ (8 November 1935) and the D 600 (10 April 1940).

Passenger cars

Leichter Personenkraftwagen (le Pkw 'o').

This was a 4x2 civilian-type light car to carry four persons but did not have a cross-country capability. The type was built by a number of companies which resulted in a variety of body styles and engine specifications, which resulted in a difference in performance.

Leichter geländegängiger Personenkraftwagen (le gl Pkw) – Kfz 1

This 4x2 light cross-country car was fitted with simple, open bodywork, with raised sides and bench-type seats; to troops in the field these resembled a bucket and it became known as the *Kübelwagen* – the name was also applied to the Volkswagen-built by *Typ* 82 which entered service in 1941. More than ten manufacturers were contracted to produce the Kfz 1.

Below:
General Guderian used a Kfz 21 medium cross-country car as his personal transport. Although appearing to be a standard vehicle, it was more comfortably equipped for use as a *Kommandeurs-Kabriolet* (commander's drop-head car) and was issued to senior commanders.

Above:
Vehicles of the *Panzerjäger-Abteilung* (PzJg-Abt – anti-tank battalion) in 12.PzDiv at a refuelling point. A BMW R12 combination is being refuelled from a 'Jerrycan' which has been supplied from a *Betriebsstoff-Wagen* (fuel wagon).

To improve off-road mobility, ground clearance was increased by fitting larger diameter balloon-type tyres.

Mittlerer Personenkraftwagen, (m Pkw 'o').
Medium-sized civilian passenger cars built by various manufacturers were procured for the army in large numbers. All received a military designation and not that of the manufacturer.

Mittlerer geländegängiger Personenkraftwagen (m gl Pkw) – Kfz 11 or Kfz 12
As with previous types, the chassis from some medium passenger cars were used as the basis for a 4x2 heavy military-pattern car with improved cross-country mobility. Vehicles fitted with a towing hook were classified as Kfz 12, those without as Kfz 11.

Schwerer Personenkraftwagen (s Pkw 'o').
These large and luxurious civilian passenger cars were mainly issued to high-ranking government officials and also senior military officers.

Schwerer geländegängiger Personenkraftwagen (s gl Pkw 'o') – Kfz 21
A number of these heavy cross-country vehicles were converted for military purposes and were often issued to staff sections. Before the war, the military had purchased a number of vehicles from various manufacturers, including six-wheeled (four driven) types. The Mercedes *Typ* G4, a 6x4 cross-country car, was frequently used by Adolf Hitler and his cohorts. The G4 was also used by high-ranking military officers.

Below:
A *Luftwaffe* Flak gun team crosses a *Brückengerät* 'B' pontoon bridge. Capacity was dependent on the length laid and varied from 8,130kg (83m) to 20,320kg (57m) and a maximum of 24,385kg (50m). Possibly for capacity reasons the gun team pulls the gun separately

Left:
The lightweight *Kübelwagen* was not easy to drive, but should it fail it was also easy to manhandle. Here troops have used steel sand mats as a ramp to load the vehicle on a standard 3-ton cargo truck.

Above:
The Czech-built Praga AV was a six-wheeled (four driven), luxuriously equipped convertible vehicle with excellent cross-country performance. Some 400 of the type, were built during the war and most were commandeered by the Germans.

Right:
The Mercedes-Benz L 1500A was one of the most effective German heavy cargo trucks: a true multi-purpose vehicle which was also used as a personnel carrier and even a light gun carrier. The L 1500A was very reliable and performed well even over rough terrain.

Passenger cars with improved cross-country performance

In the mid-1930s, an important decision was made in order to provide the army with motor vehicles having improved off-road capability. Three *Einheitsfahrgestelle* (Einh – standard) chassis types were developed: *leichter* (le – light), *mittlerer* (m – medium) and *schwere* (s – heavy). Two official designations were used for this chassis, le Pkw (E) or le Einh Pkw.

The three chassis types were fitted with bodywork for cross-country vehicles and had all-wheel drive; many were used to replace older Kfz 1, Kfz 11 or Kfz 12 and Kfz 21.

Any vehicle modified for a specific purpose would be identified by a new Kfz number. The Kfz 1 based on the new le Einh Pkw concept was manufactured by Stöwer and fitted with four-wheel drive and all-wheel steering. When it was in service as a signals or a radio vehicle it was designated Kfz 2. When armed with two *Maschinengewehr* (MG – machine gun) 34 it was classified as Kfz 4 (*leichter Truppen-Luftschutz-Kraftwagen* [le TrLSchKw – light anti-aircraft truck]). This versatile vehicle was used for a number of duties, each having an individual Kfz designation.

The m Einh Pkw was used to complement or as a substitute for all

Above:
The Mercedes-Benz G 4 was a six-wheeled (four driven) favoured by Hitler, Göring and other high-ranking Nazi officials including senior military personnel. The type was luxuriously equipped, but weighed some 3,560kg which limited cross-country performance. Both of these vehicles have been fitted with two MG 34 on pedestal-type mountings.

variants of the Kfz 11; it was designated Kfz 21 when fitted with six seats. The s Einh Pkw was used mainly as a prime mover to tow light and medium guns. The vehicle designated Kfz 69 was built by Horch and Krupp. The SdKfz 247 Ausf B armoured reconnaissance vehicle was built using the chassis of the Kfz 69.

Cargo vehicles

Military planners placed great importance on the selection of trucks for the armed forces not only as an essential means of transporting supplies, but also to carry troops and their equipment. Moving men and supplies over well-surfaced roads could be achieved by using standard civilian-type trucks, but to supply front-line forces would require a more durable type of vehicle with excellent cross-country mobility.

In the 1930s, the German army used an unimaginable diversity of truck types; almost every type available was to be found in its pre-war inventory. This made the attempt by planners to produce a classification system much more complicated than that for passenger cars.

Principally the same system as used for commercial types was followed: *leichter* (le – light), *mittlerer* (m – medium) and *schwere* (s – heavy) *Lastkraftwagen* (Lkw – cargo truck) followed by the suffix (o). Trucks with superior cross-country mobility were classified as le gl Lkw (o) and m gl Lkw (o); there were a few heavy types, but these did not enter service in significant numbers.

There were also five classes of commercial vehicle – light, medium and heavy, cross country or standard – which were used as the basis for special purpose vehicles. The cross-country types and some specialized versions also received Kfz numbers.

Below:
At the outbreak of war the Wehrmacht operated a wide variety of vehicles including numbers of commandeered civilian types. Parked by the side of the road is a Maybach luxury passenger car used by a high-ranking officer. The Vomag *Typ* 3 truck is fitted with a non-standard bodywork in place of the usual tarpaulin-covered cargo bed.
(SZ Photo)

An attempt to design a standardized truck chassis began at the same time as the Einh Pkw. However, only Henschel produced a six-wheel-drive chassis; the *Einheitsfahrgestell* le Lkw (also known as the *Einheitsdiesel*) which had excellent cross-country performance. The standard-type vehicle was built by a number of other companies including Borgward, Daimler-Benz and MAN.

Buses and other passenger carriers were mainly built on the chassis of a truck, and were again classified as light, medium and heavy. Due to having closed coachwork, the type was not only used as troop carriers, but also as command, radio and even laboratory vehicles. A number were converted to serve as ambulances.

As with the passenger car, the Kfz number issued for these trucks did not refer to the vehicle, but to its usage.

The 6x4 Krupp L2 H 143 (Kfz 69 Protze), was originally used as a towing vehicle for light (and later medium) anti-tank guns. The Horch-built Typ 40, also designated as a Kfz 69, could also be used as a replacement gun tractor.

Below:
The ex-British Morris Commercial CD, one of the many captured in good condition during the invasion of France, was often used by German forces as a replacement for the Kfz 69 as a gun tractor to tow a light anti-tank gun.

Above:
The SdKfz 10 was the most effective half-tracked tractor available which was used for numerous duties, including towing light and medium anti-tank guns. Due to the type having an excellent cross-country performance, it became the chosen vehicle of motorized units.

Left:
A Kfz 12 in service with 4.PzDiv. Although the type was mechanically complex, it was considered to be a useful vehicle by those who used it on the battlefront. Note that an MG 34 has been fitted in the pedestal mount.

Right:
It is obvious why troops named the le Pkw (o) as a *Kübelsitzewagen* (bucket seats car). The type, which had very limited cross-country performance due to it having rear-wheel drive, entered service in the 1930s but all were lost during the early part of the war.

Above:
Despite being a very good cross-country vehicle even an Einheitsdiesel could become bogged down in heavy mud. Both vehicles are *Fernsprechbetriebswagen* (telephone vehicles – Kfz 61) and are part of the signals battalion in 9.PzDiv.

Many military-pattern vehicles were often used for duties not indicated by their Kfz or SdKfz designation. Furthermore, a standard commercial light truck like the 1.5-ton Opel *Blitz* (Lightning) *Typ* 2.5-35 was purchased in large numbers, since it was cheaper to manufacture than the Kfz 69. The situation changed again; after the British evacuation at Dunkirk and the fall of France, an enormous number of serviceable trucks had been abandoned and many were taken into service by the Germans.

In the first months of the war, large numbers of civilian-owned trucks were confiscated for service with the German military, many remaining in civilian livery.

Prime movers

Unlike the situation with passenger cars and trucks, the provision of military-type prime movers followed clear specifications. A series of half-track tractors, ranging from 1-ton to 18-ton towing capacity, was purposely designed and developed for the army. All received SdKfz numbers.

le ZgKw 1 ton – SdKfz 10
le ZgKw 3 ton – SdKfz 11

m ZgKw 5 ton – SdKfz 6
m ZgKw 8 ton – SdKfz 7
s ZgKw 12 ton – SdKfz 12
s ZgKw 18 ton – SdKfz 9

As with the cross-country cars and trucks, priority was given to Panzer and motorized infantry divisions for the delivery of these highly efficient prime movers.

Armoured vehicles

Panzerspähwagen (armoured cars) were developed principally for reconnaissance and scouting roles. A small armoured car was developed using the (modified) chassis of the Horch *Typ* 108, heavy cross-country car. Soon after the *Vierrad-Panzerspähwagen* (four-wheeled armoured car) SdKfz 222, SdKfz 221 and SdKfz 223 entered service two further versions were built; a SdKfz 260, reconnaissance car and the SdKfz 261, armoured radio car. Production ended in 1943, after substantial numbers had been built, but the type continued in service until the end of the war.

A *schwerer Panzerspähwagen* (heavy armoured car), was developed at

Above:
Long before World War II, German military planners identified the value of half-tracked vehicles for highly mobile motorized units. Consequently they initiated the development of several different types from light troop carriers to heavy prime movers. Here an SdKfz 6, from an unknown unit of the artillery regiment, is in service as a gun tractor towing a 10.5cm le FH 18.

Above:
The Büssing NAG *Typ* G31 was one of the first military trucks to be delivered to the military in large numbers. Standardized as le gl Lkw (o) the vehicle had a capacity of 1,524kg. Note the *Reichswehr* licence plate remains on the vehicle.

the beginning of the 1930s using the chassis of a six-wheeled cross-country truck. Relatively small numbers of the SdKfz 231 and SdKfz 232, *Sechsrad-Panzerspähwagen* (six-wheeled armoured car) were manufactured and many of these remained in service until 1941.

The requirement to supply German formations with better, more suitable equipment resulted in a new type of heavy armoured car being developed in 1935 by Büssing-NAG: the *Typ* GS was the first purpose-built German armoured car. Known as the *Achtrad* (eight wheeled) the vehicle had very advanced transmission which provided drive and steering to all wheels, resulting in superb cross-country performance. The type had a driving position at the front and another at the rear. Due to its size, a wide variety of radio equipment could be installed. These vehicles were standardized as the SdKfz 231 and SdKfz 232.

Production of the *Typ* GS ended in 1943 and was replaced by the Tatra-powered ARK type SdKfz 234/1; a far more effective vehicle. Almost immediately the SdKfz 234/3 armed with 7.5cm StuK L/24 gun entered service and a number (SdKfz 234/4) were mounted with 7.5cm PaK 40 anti-tank gun.

The superstructure on both types was fabricated using a complicated assembly of sloped-armour plating which gave the crew protection against armour-piercing infantry bullets.

Although a type of armoured carrier had been developed in France before the war, Germany was the first nation to introduce a *Schützenpanzerwagen* (armoured personnel carrier) into regular service. It was the intention of military planners to equip all *Schützen-Regimenter* (rifle regiments) in the Panzer divisions with the type, but the situation in Germany caused production of this versatile vehicle to commence at a very slow pace. For the invasion of Poland, 1.PzDiv received a limited number of the type and the situation had not changed significantly when German forces invaded France. Here the discrepancy in the numbers published in the relative KStN and those available is obvious.

Tanks

From the beginning of the *Panzerwaffe*, it was planned to introduce two types of tank; the *Zugführerwagen* (ZW – platoon commander's vehicle) as the main battle tank, and the *Battailonsführerwagen* (BW – battalion commander's vehicle) to monitor the battlefield.

However, due to the strict financial constraints placed on Germany military planners decided to equip the first armoured formations with a

Below:
The SdKfz 221, *leichter Panzerspähwagen* (le PzSpWg – light armoured vehicle), was issued to a number of reconnaissance battalions, but due to the type being armed with an MG 34 and not fitted with radio equipment it soon became obsolete.

Left:
A number of German tank
units were equipped
with Czech-built vehicles
commandeered after the
occupation. One such unit
was 6.PzDiv which received
the LT vz 35; the type was
re-designated as the PzKpfw
35(t). The tank was used
extensively during the initial
phases of *Unternehmen*
(operation) Barbarossa.
Note the radio operator and
his Torn FuG 'b1' portable
transceiver in a dug-in
position.

Below:
As the number of serviceable PzKpfw 35(t) diminished, German military planners decided that the production of the LT vz 38 (later PzKpfw 38[t]) would be continued. The type, armed with a 3.7cm KwK 38(t) L/47.8 manufactured by Škoda, replaced the PzKpfw III in five Panzer divisions (as of June 1941). The PzKpfw 38(t) could not defeat the Soviet T-34 and consequently was slowly phased out of German front-line service.

cheap and mechanically simple light tank. The PzKpfw I was built using the chassis of the *Landwirtschaftlicher-Ackerschlepper* (LaS – agricultural tractor) and armed with two *Maschinengewehr* (MG – machine gun) 34. The type was used to train thousands of tank crews, the backbone of all future tank divisions. [*History of the Panzerwaffe: Volume One*, Osprey 2015]

Fiscal and other problems delayed the development and, ultimately, the procurement of a main battle tank. The situation forced planners to order another type of light tank, the LaS-100, for service in 1935/36. Designated PzKpfw II, the type was armed with a 2cm gun and an MG 34. It would remain in front-line service until sufficient PzKpfw III and PzKpfw IV became available to front-line units; then it would be used for reconnaissance and support duties.

After the annexation of Czechoslovakia, German forces discovered two very useful tank types which had been destined for service with the Czech army. Almost immediately German military planners ordered both types

to be mass produced. This allowed planners to order the establishment of another two Panzer divisions before the outbreak of the war.

In 1939, German armoured forces now had six tank types in active service instead of the planned two:

PzKpfw I	(LaS)
PzKpfw II	(LaS-100)
PzKpfw III	(ZW)
PzKpfw IV	(BW)
PzKpfw 35(t)	(Czech-built LT vz 35)
PzKpfw 38(t)	(Czech-built LT vz 38)

Command tank variants – equipped with dedicated radio equipment, but no main armament – of the PzKpfw III, PzKpfw 35(t) and PzKpfw 38(t) were developed.

Above:
June 1940: a number of PzKpfw 35(t) of 6.PzDiv advancing across a field of cereals during the invasion of France. Although the tank was considered to be reliable (except in very cold conditions) and had good cross-country performance, it was too lightly armed and soon became obsolete.

Above:
Before the war a number of heavy armoured vehicles were built to be used as armoured staff cars. One such type, the SdKfz 247 Ausf B, was issued to the staff section of the reconnaissance battalion in 6.PzDiv. The vehicle was not originally fitted with radio equipment, but this was quickly rectified.

Leading a Panzer division

Leading a large formation such as a Panzer division required effective communications. The German authorities recognized this problem early having realized that tanks and other combat vehicles (as the spearhead of an attack) would rely on radios rather than flags to communicate. Planners ordered that the design and development of more sophisticated and reliable radio equipment was to be expedited. A requirement was issued for each tank in a combat company to be fitted with a radio receiver, and those of a platoon or company commander were to have a receiver and a transmitter (transceiver). For the effective leadership at battalion and regimental level, each command tank would be fitted with long-range radio equipment.

Radio communications on platoon and company level

In 1940, an extensive list was published detailing the enormous number of different radio installations available to communications units. From the day they were established, German armed forces had been equipped with effective radios (transmitters, receivers or transceivers) for battlefield communications. This equipment was the responsibility of a relatively small sections known as *Funktrupp* (radio troop) which were classified according to their role and the equipment they operated: *kleiner* (small), *mittlerer* (medium) and *Großer* (large) *Funktrupp*. In 1943, these were changed to keep in line with contemporary German classification: *leichter Funktrupp* (le FuTrp – light radio troop); *mittlerer Funktrupp* (m FuTrp – medium radio troop) and *schwerer Funktrupp* (s FuTrp – heavy radio troop). Each of these categories was again classified by a suffix to identify the type and range of the equipment. Armoured radio sections were available to all sections.

[To simplify identification original designations are used: 'E' – *Empfänger* (receiver), 'S' – *Sender* (transmitter) and 'U' – *Umformer* (converter)].

The *kleiner Panzer-Funktrupp* (mot) 'c' (kl PzFuTrp – light armoured radio section [motorized]) was issued with an SdKfz 261 fitted with a 20W S 'd' and an Fu 7, *Ultra-Kurz Welle* (UKW – ultra-short wave) for air-to-ground communication. The vehicle had a 2m *Stabantenne* (rod-type aerial) which allowed – voice and Morse – transmissions of up to 80km.

The kl PzFuTrp (mot) 'd' was issued with an SdKfz 261 fitted with a 30W S 'a' and two Torn E 'b' for long-range communications. The vehicle was fitted with a frame-type aerial, but also carried an 8m extending-type aerial.

The *mittlerer Panzer-Funktrupp* (mot) 'b' (m PzFuTrp – medium armoured radio section) was issued with a Kfz 15 and also an SdKfz 263 (*Achtrad* – eight wheeled) armoured car – the type was a dedicated radio vehicle and had a fixed superstructure mounting a frame-type aerial. The section was issued with a Fu 11 SE 100 radio set: a 100W *Sender* and a portable Torn *Emphänger* 'b'. The section was also issued with a second Torn E 'b'.

Left:
This ex-British Morris Commercial CS 8 fitted with a cargo body is being used by a German unit as a telephone cable-layer vehicle. Note the cable reels mounted on the mudguards.

The SdKfz 263 also carried a 9m extending-type aerial which increased maximum transmission range to 70km (200km Morse).

All the above PzFuTrp (mot) sections could also use soft-skinned vehicles to carry the radio equipment.

In late 1940, an improved radio was introduced to gradually replace the Fu 11 SE 100 which equipped all *mittlerer Panzer-Funktrupp* (mot) 'b' sections. Although the new Fu 12 SE 80 was rated at 80W it had the same performance as the Fu 11.

One of the mainstays of the German army was the *Funk-Kraftwagen* (Fu-Kw – radio car) Kfz 15 which could be fitted with seven different types of radio installation; the smaller Kfz 2 was available with eight types of installation. It is most probable that the extensive list of installations could easily be increased, since troops in the field assembled, modified or converted any available radio equipment.

In 1940, the tank element in a Panzer division and attached units were equipped as follows:

Fu 2 EU
This *Ultra-Kurz Welle* (UKW – ultra-short wave) radio consisted of an *Empfänger* 'e' fitted with a matching *Umformer*.

Below:
The Panzer divisions utilized a wide variety of passenger vehicles. The Büssing-NAG 900 N *schwerer Kraftomnibus* (s Kom – heavy passenger bus) was one such type and was often used for special services requiring space and cleanliness.

Fu 5 SE10 U

A UKW radio with an *Empfänger* 'e', a 10W *Sender* 'c' and a *Unformer*, which had a voice range of 2km (moving) and 3km (static); by using Morse code telegraphy, a 25 per cent improvement in range was possible.

Initial long-term planning stated that every tank in a combat company was to be fitted with Fu 5 and Fu 2 radios. This proved to be impossible, which meant that until 1942 most tanks in a platoon were fitted with a Fu 2, and the platoon leader a Fu 5.

Both the Fu 5 and Fu 2 were connected to a 2m *Stabantenne* (rod antenna).

Fu 6 SE 20 U

This UKW set included the 20W *Sender* 'c' and *Empfänger* 'e' with an *Unformer*. Due to the higher performance of the transmitter, voice range increased to 6km. The Fu 6 operated with a 2m *Stabantenne* (rod aerial).

Initially company commanders were provided with *kleine Panzerbefehlswagen* (kl PzBefWg – light commander's vehicle – SdKfz 265) equipped with Fu 6 and Fu 2 radios. In 1939, the kl PzBefWg began to be replaced by the PzKpfw III and PzKpfw IV which were equipped with Fu 5 and Fu 2. Those SdKfz 265

Above:
A Kfz 17/1 in service with the kl FuTrp 'c' (light radio section) of the signals battalion in 15.PzDiv; this type of vehicle was also used by the signals and artillery units in a Panzer division during the war in the desert.

that did remain in service continued to be used for command duties in staff sections, indeed some were still on the battlefront in 1944.

The Fu 6 radio was also fitted in the *schwere Panzerbefehlswagen* (s PzBefWg – heavy commander's vehicle – SdKfz 266). It is thought that only a few of the type were built; the performance of the standard tanks equipped with Fu 5 and Fu 2 radios was considered adequate. Subsequently, the SdKfz 266 was only issued to battalion and regimental staff sections.

Command echelons

Long-range radio communication was vitally important: The Fu 8 SE 30 medium wave (MW) radio included a 30W *Sender* and an *Empfänger* 'c' with *Unformer*. In a static location, the equipment had a voice range of 50km (150km Morse) using a telescopic mast mounted with a *Sterantenne* (star antenna); on the march, a voice range of 15km (40km Morse) was achievable by utilizing the frame-type antenna mounted at the rear over the engine compartment. A further Fu 6 radio completed the equipment.

This radio was also mounted in the *grosser* PzBefWg (SdKfz 267) in service with brigade, battalion and regimental staffs.

Fu 7 SE 20 U

The *Luftwaffe* battlefield liaison officers had special radio equipment to allow air-to-ground communication. The UKW radio consisted of a 20W *Sender* 'd' and a *Empfänger* 'd1'. Normally used only in static position with a 1.4m rod antenna, the transmitter had a voice range of 50km (100km

Right:
Radio sections such as a kl FuTrp 'b' (mot), were usually carried in a Kfz 17 which was equipped with an MS EG 400 portable generator. But if the supply of electricity failed a member of the team would have to operate a pedal-powered auxiliary generator.

Morse) and 500m range for air-to-ground contact. The Fu 7 and a Fu 6 were also fitted in the s PzBefWg (now designated SdKfz 268) and used by brigade, battalion and regimental staff sections.

The SdKfz 266, 267 and 268 were manufactured as one basic version. But like combat tanks, they would be delivered to *Heereszeugämter* (army depots) where they would be fitted with armament, ammunition, tools and radio equipment.

Panzerdivision as of 1940 – Provision of Signals Elements with Radios: Interoperability

	Panzer	Schützen gep	Schützen ungep	Artillerie	Pioniere gep	Pioniere ungep	Panzerjäger	AufklAbt	Heeresflieger
Brigade	Fu 12								
	Fu 8	Fu 8	Fu 8	Fu 8					
	Fu 6	Fu 5							
	Fu 7	Fu 7	Fu 3	Fu 7					Fu 7
Regiment	Fu 12								
	Fu 8	Fu 8	Fu 8	Fu 8					
		Torn FuG b	Torn FuG b						
	Fu 5, Fu 6	Fu 5							
		FuSprech f							
	Fu 7	Fu 7	Fu 7	Fu 7					
Bataillon (Abteilung)	Fu 12							Fu 12	Fu 12
	Fu 8	Fu 8	Fu 8	Fu 8	Fu 8	Fu 8	Fu 8		Fu 8
		Torn FuG b	Torn FuG b	Torn FuG b					
	Fu 5, Fu 6 FeldFuSpr f	Fu 5 FuSprech f			FuSprech f	Feld FuSprech f	Feld FuSprech f	Feld FuSprech f	
	Fu 7			Fu 7				Fu 7	
Kompanie (Batterie)		Fu 8		Fu 8					
		Torn FuG b	Torn FuG b	Torn FuG b	Torn FuG b		Torn FuG b	Torn FuG b	Torn FuG b
	Fu 5			Feld FuSprech f	Fu 5 Feld FuSprech f	Feld FuSprech f		Fu 5 Feld FuSprech f	
		FuSprech f		FuSprech f	FuSprech f			FuSprech a	
		Feld FuSprech b	Feld FuSprech b		Feld FuSprech b	Feld FuSprech b		Feld FuSprech b	
Zug (Platoon)								Fu 12	
	Fu 5	Feld FuSprech f	Feld FuSprech f		Feld FuSprech f			Feld FuSprech f	
		FuSprech f			FuSprech f			FuSprech a	
		Feld FuSprech b	Feld FuSprech b		Feld FuSprech b	Feld FuSprech b		Feld FuSprech b	

CHAPTER 3

THE PANZER DIVISION

Ideally, the new armoured divisions were to be formed according to the inventories published in the *Kriegstärkenachweisungen* (KStN – tables of organization). But due to the ever-present problems facing the Reich these organizational documents could never be implemented let alone complied with. Furthermore they were subjected to regular changes based on organizational and supply problems and were altered as soon as after-action reports from front-line units had been evaluated.

The first tables of organization for the tank divisions were published in 1934. In principle, these should remain effective until end of the war. However, in the process of building up the new military, those in charge had to react and make permanent changes.

Financial and material restrictions were omnipresent in the pre-war years and due to a lack of experience, the standard method of tackling a problem was by trial and error or by improvising using all available resources. A rigid timetable had been set and no effort would be spared to meet the deadline.

The number of tanks, the most vital element of the division, increased and gradually reached a peak in mid-1939.

In 1935, three Panzer divisions were established and a further three were formed before the outbreak of the war:

1.PzDiv (Weimar)
2.PzDiv (Würzburg)
3.PzDiv (Wünsdorf)
4.PzDiv (Würzburg)

Left:
The commander of 7.PzDiv, Erwin Rommel in a *großer Panzerbefehlswagen* (SdKfz 267) discusses map references with a senior officer from his brigade staff. Although the rod-type aerial appeared to be a substantial item it was extremely fragile and easily damaged.

Above:
An SdKfz 263 (Fu) radio car from a medium armoured radio section 'a' and 'b'; the unit was equipped with a 100W transmitter and two Torn E 'b' receivers. Most SdKfz 263 were issued to reconnaissance and single units in a Panzer division.

5.PzDiv (Oppeln)
10.PzDiv (Prague)

In principle, the organization of all the divisions was to have been identical; each having four Panzer battalions. However, 10.PzDiv had only two Panzer battalions – half the authorized strength.

The table on page 72 concerns 1.PzDiv at the beginning of *Fall Gelb* (Plan Yellow) – the invasion of France – and are only an indication of the true position and bear some inaccuracies.

Command structure

A military unit as large as a Panzer division was dependent on an effective command structure, essential for successful combat operations.

The Panzer division of 1935 had a staff section for every level of command:

Divisionsstab (divisional staff)
Brigadestab (brigade staff) – for tank and rifle brigade.

Regimentsstab (regimental staff) – for tank and rifle brigade.
Bataillonsstab (battalion staff) – for all battalions.
Kompaniestab (company staff) – for all companies.

This basic organization was in position at the beginning of the war. But in the summer of 1940 after the fall of France, and despite the existence of organizational structures, no Panzer division was identical in manpower and equipment. Shortfalls in production, which led to varying availability during the establishment phase, were accepted as normal, forcing all units to adapt each KStN according their actual allocation of equipment. This ability to adapt was essential for survival on the battlefield when equipment was damaged or destroyed by enemy action or suffered mechanical failure.

[Note: Numerous contemporary documents were researched for this book including a very detailed file assembled by 6.PzDiv. It details every single vehicle from all levels of staff section to the lowest level combat units. Unfortunately, this unit is not a perfect example from which to confirm the organizational structure of a 'typical' Panzer division. In 1940, 6.PzDiv had only three battalions in the Panzer brigade and this unit was part of the three units being equipped with Czech-built tanks; the medium tanks were replaced by PzKpfw 35(t). Similarly, 7.PzDiv and 8.PzDiv were equipped with the PzKpfw 38(t) instead of the PzKpfw III.]

Below:
Luxurious passenger cars manufactured by companies including Horch, Maybach and Mercedes Benz were issued to senior officers at the highest level of command.

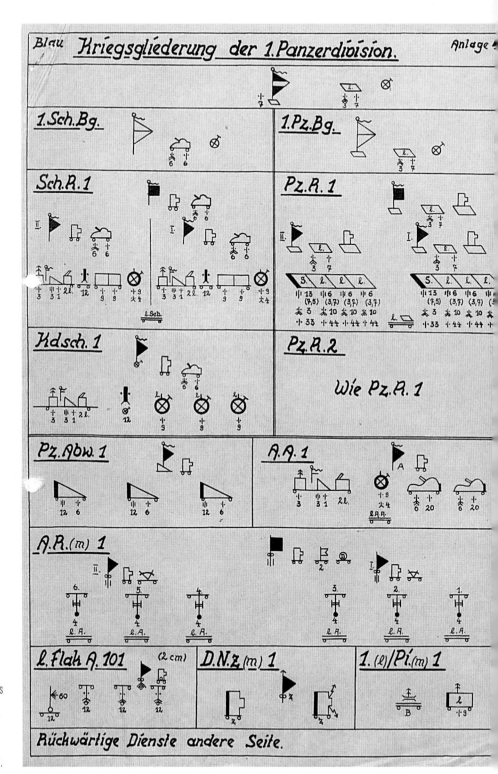

Right:
The proposed structure of 1.PzDiv as published in 1934 shows a force of 52 7.5cm-armed PzKpfw IV tanks and 3.7cm-armed 72 PzKpfw III tanks. Also there are over 100 PzKpfw I and PzKpfw II light tanks. In reality these figures were never achieved.

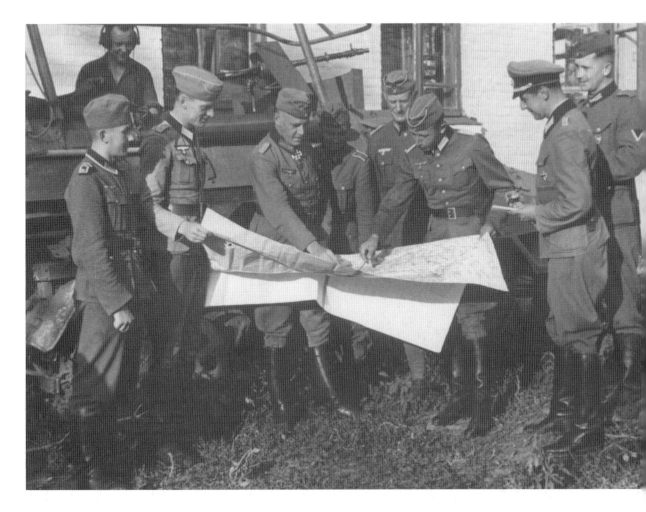

Staff echelon

KStN 51 describes the *Kommando einer Panzerdivision:* the highest level in the command structure, manned by commissioned officers, NCOs and conscripts from different branches in the division. In combat, the tactical group would be located some 10 to 15km behind the front-line positions with the offices of the adjutant and the quartermaster even further to the rear. The divisional commander would be close to his troops in the frontline and supported by the *Ordonnanzoffizier* (special missions officer) and the divisional artillery liaison officer from his *Führungsstaffel* (lead squadron). Personnel strength was 19 officers, 11 officials, 38 NCOs and 117 conscripts.

Division commander

Usually holding the rank of general, the *Divisionskommandeur* (divisional commander) was the staff officer with overall responsibility. He issued

Above:
The SdKfz 251/6 armoured command vehicles was fitted with long-range radio equipment such as the 80W S transmitter. The large frame-type antenna, necessary for the radio to function, proved to be too conspicuous. From 1942, it was replaced by the *Sterantenne* (star antenna).

Left:
On 20 April 1939, German forces assembled on the *Ostwestache*, Berlin for a parade to celebrate the 50th birthday of Adolf Hitler. To achieve a maximum degree of strategic mobility, tank units were equipped with heavy trucks and flat-bed trailers. This concept did not prove satisfactory and was abandoned in early 1940. (Getty)

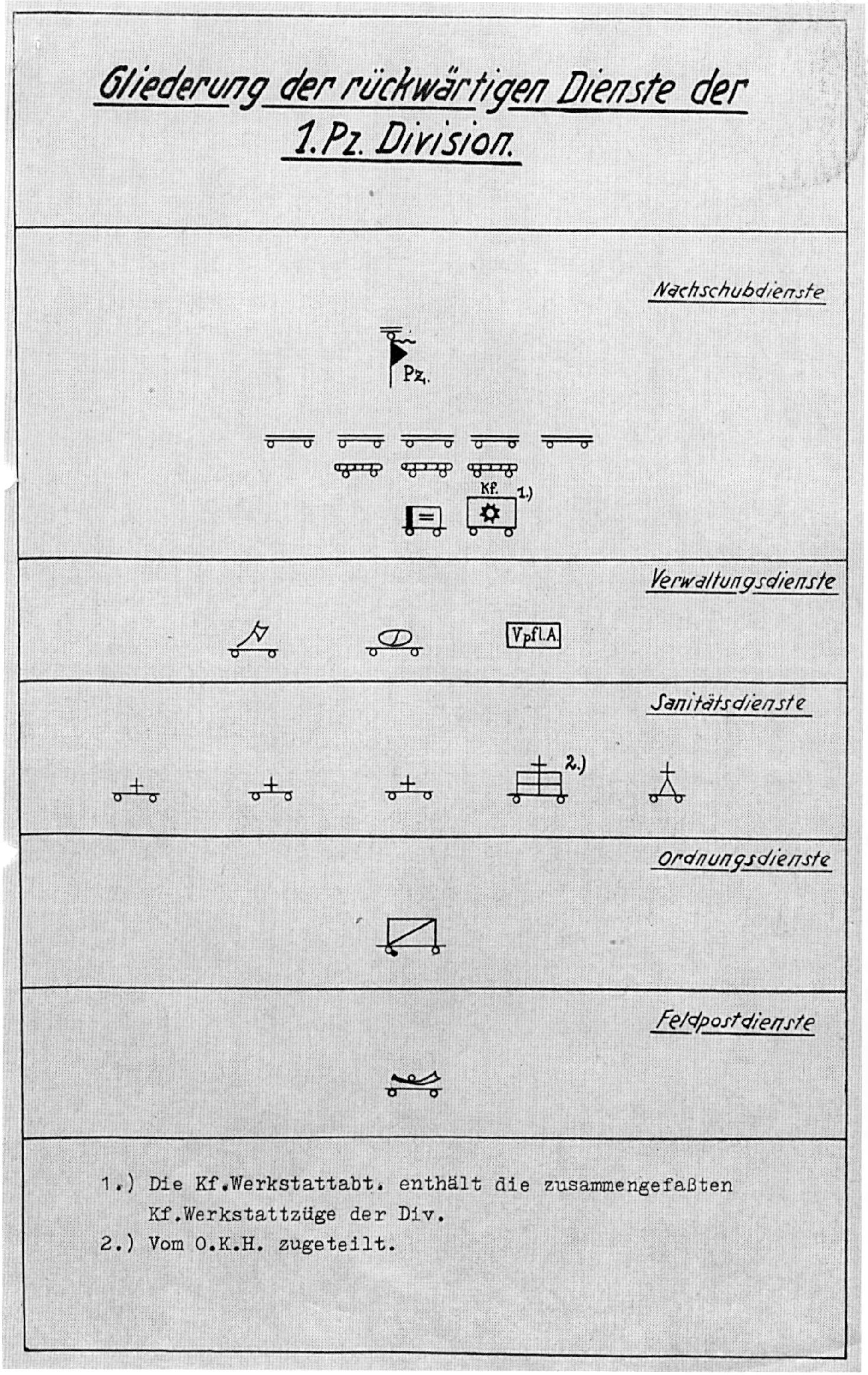
Gliederung der rückwärtigen Dienste der 1.Pz. Division.
Nachschubdienste
Pz.
Kf.
1.)
Verwaltungsdienste
Vpfl.A.
Sanitätsdienste
2.)
Ordnungsdienste
Feldpostdienste
1.) Die Kf.Werkstattabt. enthält die zusammengefaßten Kf.Werkstattzüge der Div.
2.) Vom O.K.H. zugeteilt.

Right:
The proposed support units of 1.PzDiv as published in 1934.

combat orders and was responsible for all equipment and the well-being of his personnel.

Tactical group

The *Führungs-Abteilung* (tactical group) was led by the *Erster Generalstabsoffizier* (first general staff officer), who was responsible for the deployment of combat forces. The *Ordonnanzoffizier* (special missions officer) was responsible for keeping maps and the war diary up to date. His assistant, aided by interpreters, collated all intelligence – including interrogations – regarding enemy forces and their positions on the battlefront.

The divisional artillery liaison officers, the engineer battalion and the tactical group signals battalion and other units attached to the division, were also part of the tactical group.

Quartermaster group

The *zweite Generalstabsoffizier* (second general staff officer) commanded the *Quartiermeister-Abteilung* (quartermaster battalion) and was responsible for the supply and replenishment of the division.

Below:
During the French campaign *Oberstleutnant* Koppenburg, the commander of PzRgt 1 in 1.PzDiv, temporarily used a PzKpfw IV Ausf A. An odd choice, since the tank had only basic radio equipment and lacked armour protection.

Above:
The kl PzBefWg (SdKfz 265) was initially used by leaders of light and medium tank companies until being replaced by tanks. The type was then fitted with long-range radio equipment before being issued to PzDiv staff and signals sections. This SdKfz 265 vehicle has been fitted with a non-standard frame-type antenna.

There were four staff officers; engineers who were responsible for motor vehicles, ammunition and weapons; and others who organized the supply and baggage train.

The *Divisionsintendant* was responsible for keeping the division supplied with food, clothing, accommodation and other essentials.

The *Divisionsarmsatz* (divisional medical officer) was responsible for the general health of the personnel, the recovery and treatment of the wounded, and organized the supply of essential medicines.

The *Zahlmeister* (paymaster) led the accounting office and ensured that all personnel were paid.

Adjutant

The office of the *Adjudantur* (adjutant) was responsible for the personnel in the division and organizing replacement personnel when required.

The Padre took care of all matters religious and spiritual.

The *Divisionsjustizbeamter* (divisional judicial officer) was the head of the military court and was responsible for all disciplinary matters.

Table KStN 51 lists only a very basic provision with motor vehicles – when required extra vehicles would be commandeered from other divisional subunits, the largest number coming from the *Panzernachrichten-Abteilung* (armoured signals battalion). The divisional commander was authorized to request more men and equipment, mainly from the reconnaissance and signals units.

The division commander was normally provided with a Kfz 21 heavy passenger car for transport, but in 1940 he would be provided with a 6x4 cross-country vehicle; but this would be subject to availability.

A number of light and heavy passenger cars, all 4x2 driven, were also distributed. Only five cross-country cars were delivered, including the Kfz 2/40 for the workshop section.

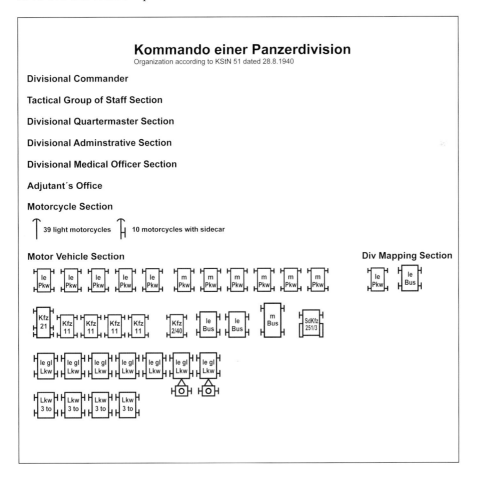

Seven 1.5-ton light trucks and four 3-ton medium trucks were available for the transport of fuel, baggage and food. Two would be used for towing the *Feldküche* (field kitchen).

Three civilian-type passenger coaches were available, some reworked to provide office space for HQ personnel.

The only armoured vehicle on the divisional staff was a *mittlerer Schützenpanzerwagen mit Funknachrichtengerät* (m SPw – medium personnel carrier with radio equipment). In 1940, no specific variant of the SdKfz 251 had been produced to carry long-range radio equipment, so a standard SdKfz 251 was modified for this purpose.

In early 1941, the SdKfz 251/6 (*mittlerer Kommandopanzerwagen* – medium command vehicle) entered service and, for reasons unknown, a year later another communications version was introduced. The new *mittlerer Funkpanzerwagen* (medium radio vehicle) was designated SdKfz 251/3. The SdKfz 251/6 is no longer listed in documents dating from 1944, but many of these vehicles continued in service with staff sections.

The unit was supplied with 49 motorcycles which were mainly used by dispatch riders.

Below:
In 1943, work began to modify the PzKpfw IV to command tank specification using production tanks or refurbished battle-worn vehicles. This PzBefWg IV Ausf J is in service with 2.PzDiv in France, 1944.

Left:
In the North African desert Rommel used an SdKfz 250/3, fitted with identical radio equipment as in the SdKfz 251/6, as his personal transport. He named the vehicle '*Greif*' (Griffon).

Below:
To improve the performance of the long-range radios fitted in the SdKfz 251/6, all were fitted with the telescopic-type mast: an 8m version for the 80W S transmitter and 9m for the 100W S transmitter. It is almost certain that both were interchangeable.

Above:
Early versions of the PzBefWg III were fitted with a large, conspicuous frame-type antenna which made it easy for the enemy to identify; the vehicle was always treated as a prime target. Later versions such as the PzBefWg III Ausf K were fitted with less prominent *Sterantenne* (star antenna) and mounted a 5cm KwK 39 L/60. These command tanks are in service with PzGrenDiv Großdeutschland.

The mapping section of the divisional staff (organized according KStN 2076), was supplied with a passenger coach equipped as an office and also a light motor car.

Panzer brigade staff

To bring the two Panzer regiments (PzRgt) within the Panzer division, a further organizational level was created, the *Panzerbrigade* (PzBrig – tank brigade). By definition a brigade, the smallest element in a larger formation, must be capable of offensive operations; an ideal unit for the German assault tactics. In the formation phase of the *Panzerwaffe*, this was the simplest way to put larger tank forces under a clear chain of command with the aim of concentrating the main tank effort at a focal point on the frontline and achieve a rapid breakthrough. When the two Panzer regiments were deployed as a combined force, the brigade commander would take control and organize a reconnaissance of the front. Following orders from the divisional commander and using reconnaissance information, he would lead his force in the attack.

In 1935, six brigades were established, and the first three were attached to 1.PzDiv, 2.PzDiv and 3.PzDiv. The remaining three operated as independent units until they were attached to newly established Panzer divisions.

A brigade was formed as two Panzer regiments, each with two Panzer battalions of eight (four each) companies.

This composition was repeatedly questioned, since it remained untried. During the invasion of France, 7.PzDiv trialled alternative structures:

PzBrig with two PzRgt having three PzAbt each of three Panzer-Kompanie (PzKp – tank company): a total of 18 companies.

Instead of the PzBrig only one PzRgt with three PzAbt having four PzKp each: a total of 12 companies.

In the latter part of 1940, the general staff decided to keep the original composition (16 companies).

The brigade staff was small – four officers, six NCOs and 24 conscripts – and was organized according KStN 53, dated 1 October 1937. The brigade staff was issued with a small number of soft-skinned vehicles.

Below:
Anti-aircraft protection was vital for every military unit, especially in the wide openness of the North African desert. Here an MG 34 is fitted with an anti-aircraft type gunsight and mounted on a sturdy tripod.

Left:
France, 1940: two *Achtrad* (eight-wheeled) SdKfz 263 *Panzerfunkwagen* (armoured radio cars) cross a bridge assembled from two *Übergangsschienen* (portable bridge sections) of a *Brückengerät* 'K'. The operation is being covered by a camouflaged PzKpfw II; note the anti-aircraft machine gun.

Right:
In 1939, the PzKpfw II was the main light tank in German service, but it was soon being gradually withdrawn from front-line duties. Instead it was used as a liaison or scouting vehicle or to transport ammunition. Here a PzKpfw II Ausf C from 4.PzDiv crosses a stretch of small tree trunks laid over soft ground during the advance into Poland, 1939.

For communication the PzBrig commander relied on the divisional PzNachrAbt. But depending on orders from divisional HQ and the situation, *Panzerbefehlswagen* (PzBefWg – command tank) could be requested along with other radio vehicles should the situation become difficult.

In 1940, the number of battalions in Panzer divisions was reduced from four to two, and the brigade was dropped, but with the exception of 3.PzDiv (PzBrig 5).

Panzer regiment staff

The first five Panzer divisions, established before 1939, each had two Panzer regiments and, according to KStN 1103, each had a staff and also a staff company, with a complement of eight officers, one official, 47 NCOs and 66 conscripts.

Provision with soft-skinned vehicles was, as always, subject to availability. A set of files collated by 6.PzDiv in February 1940, identifies their vehicles by class (e.g. le gl Pkw) rather than Kfz numbers.

Below:
May 1941: A long column of German vehicles, carrying personnel from the port of Derna, Libya, slowly climb a mountain road on the way to link up with combat units. British forces have abandoned a Cruiser Tank Mk 1 (A9) and a Daimler Scout Car during their retreat. (Getty)

Left:
Unternehmen (Operation) Barbarossa was supposed to be completed within a few weeks, but due to resolute resistance by Soviet forces the advance slowed into autumn. For almost five months the road conditions had been good; then rains came and with them a nightmare for German logistic services. As winter arrived the heavy mud froze and was then covered in a thick blanket of snow. Horse-drawn transport was often the last means for supply, being able to move under almost all conditions. (Getty)

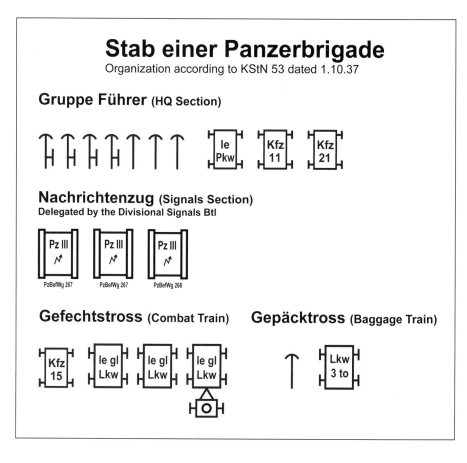

In 1940, a regimental commander was supplied with a medium cross-country vehicle, usually a Kfz 15. His staff officers would have the use of medium and heavy cars, possibly including the Kfz 21. Six motorcycles were also issued.

The transport train had several motor cars and five 1.5-ton trucks: the rations and baggage trains had a similar allocation. The small workshop troop was supplied with a medium cross-country car. The medical troop had a *mittlerer Kraftomnibus* (m Kom – medium passenger coach) which they used as an auxiliary ambulance.

Since the regimental staff would be very close to the battalions during a battle, a *leichter Panzer-Zug* (le Pz Zug – light tank platoon), to KStN 1168, and a signals platoon, to KStN 1194, were also included.

In 1939, the light tank platoon would be formed with five PzKpfw II. This shows the pace of progress: two years earlier the platoon had one kl PzBefWg, two PzKpfw I and two PzKpfw II. The light platoon would be called on to perform reconnaissance, security tasks and liaison duties.

Left:
All PzBefWg III (SdKfz 267) equipped with Fu 8 radios that were issued to the staff and signals section of a Panzer division were usually fitted with the frame-type antenna. This could be replaced by a telescopic-type aerial mounted on the top of the turret which, under favourable conditions, could treble the range to 60km (voice) and 120km (Morse).

Right:
1940: A column of vehicles, including passenger coaches, from a signals battalion during the advance through The Low Countries. A number of vehicles are draped with an orange flag as a recognition aid for patrolling aircraft. (Getty)

Above:
The commander of a PzBefWg III from III./PzRgt 25 in 7.PzDiv in discussion with senior officers. Note the extra 'Jerrycans' of fuel on the engine deck; vital during the advance in Russia.

The signals platoon was an essential part of the staff company and provided contact between the regimental staff and higher and lower levels of command, including the battalions. The platoon was issued with a PzKpfw III, armed with a 3.7cm KwK L/45, and two SdKfz 267 Ausf B, armoured command cars. For air-to-ground communications an SdKfz 268 would be made available. A number of radio sections carried in soft-skinned vehicles would be spread across the battlefront.

The platoon was also issued with Kfz 15 cross-country cars. The platoon leader, two radio sections and the two telephone cable-laying sections were also issued with the Kfz 15.

Under normal circumstances, the regimental commander and his deputy were issued with command tanks deployed by the divisional PzNachrAbt. Occasionally, a PzKpfw III armed with a 3.7cm KwK L/45 was deployed for defensive duties.

Stab eines Panzerregiments
Organization according to KStN 1103 dated 1.11.41

Gruppe Führer (Regimental HQ)

| Kfz 12 | Kfz 15 | Kfz 15 | m Pkw | s Pkw | Kfz 21 |

Light Tank Platoon

| Pz II | Pz II | Pz II | Pz II | Pz II | le gl Lkw |

Signals Platoon

| Kfz 15 | Kfz 15 | Kfz 15 | Kfz 15 | Kfz 15 | le gl Lkw | Pz III | PzBef III PzBefWg 267 | PzBef III PzBefWg 267 |

Gefechtstross (Combat Train)

| le Pkw | Kfz 12 | le gl Lkw | le gl Lkw | le gl Lkw | le gl Lkw | le gl Lkw |

Verpflegungstross (Rations Train)

| le Pkw | le gl Lkw | m gl Lkw |

Gepäcktross Baggage Train

| m gl Lkw |

Instandsetzungsstaffel Workshop Section

| m Pkw |

Krankentrupp Medical Section

| m Bus |

Left:
Command tanks of a Panzer brigade staff: An 8m *Kurbelmast* (telescopic mast) has been erected on the PzBefWg III for long-range communications. The kl PzBefWg is operating as a relay to lower divisional echelons.

Panzer Battalion Staff

The two PzAbt in a PzRgt had almost identical staff sections – KStN 1107 details the battalion staff section, KStN 1150 the staff company. [Note: Since no KStN from 1940 survive, information published in tables relating to 6.PzDiv has been used.] These very detailed documents show again that the higher level staffs were authorized to adapt the tables to suit their own requirements or whims.

The battalion staff section was almost comparable to that of a Panzer regiment. However, in the case of regimental staff support services, such as the light tank platoon or the signals platoon, were directly subordinate to the staff section. In contrast, the battalion had a separate staff company which controlled its own reconnaissance and engineer platoons.

However, 6.PzDiv showed a deviation to the structure. Instead of providing the staff section with the minimum of necessary vehicles, it shows that a rations and combat train was established. Somewhat oddly, the workshop section was larger than that of the staff company.

The signals platoon, an essential part of the staff company, provided the means to establish and maintain contact between the combat companies, and also the command echelons. The platoon was issued with a PzKpfw III

and two radio-equipped command tanks: many sources indicate that these were SdKfz 266, but it is equally possible that they were radio-equipped SdKfz 267 command tanks.

In mid-1940, the light platoon was equipped with six PzKpfw II, which they used for scouting, liaison and security. The reconnaissance platoon was motorcycle mounted and had a dispatch rider section and four reconnaissance sections.

The engineer platoon was able to provide all types of mechanical assistance, and a number of specialists with equipment to clear mines and other obstacles.

The anti-aircraft platoon was issued with four *leichte Truppenluftschutzwagen*, (light anti-aircraft vehicles) built on the Kfz 4 and armed with two MG 34 in a *Zwillings-Socksllafette* (ZwiSoLe – twin mounting).

The battalion staff in the medical section was supplied with a Kfz 31 *Krankenwagen* (ambulance), whereas the staff company was issued with a motorcycle and a combination.

The staff section of a tank battalion was manned by seven officers, two officials, seven NCOs and 14 conscripts. The tank battalion staff company had a complement of three officers, 35 NCOs and 107 conscripts.

Below:
France, 1940: members of a PzAbt observe the progress of a battle. A SdKfz 221 armoured car, which was used for liaison or scouting duties, is positioned alongside the PzBefWg III.

Above:
The PzBefWg III Ausf J was the first version to have the replica gun replaced by a 5cm KwK 39 L/60 tank gun. The tank has been fitted with *Seitenschürzen* (side skirts) by workshop engineers in preparation for the Kursk campaign in July 1943.

Problems

As stated previously, some of the individual staff sections received equipment and personnel seconded from other subunits in the divisions.

According to its KStN, the PzNachAbt had five SdKfz 267 command tanks and two SdKfz 268 for the *Fliegerverbindungs-Offizier* (FliVO – ground-to-air liaison officer). Documents suggest that three other command tanks were to be seconded to the divisional brigade staff. All other staff units were to have their own armoured signals elements according the respective various KStNs.

According to the valid KStN, all command tanks from different staff sections – eight SdKfz 266, six SdKfz 267 and two SdKfz 268 – were to be issued to complete a Panzer division.

The total number of command tanks available to all ten Panzer divisions in June 1940 can be traced through documents. The table shows that only 1.PzDiv and 7.PzDiv did not receive this allotment, but the majority did and some exceeded the allotment. However, only some 75 PzKpfw III heavy command tanks had been produced by May 1940, making it possible that the missing PzBefWg were replaced by surplus SdKfz 265. These had originally been used at company level and were fitted with compatible radio equipment.

There is some uncertainty: 6.PzDiv, 7.PzDiv and 8.PzDiv were not issued with PzKpfw III command tanks, but with Czech-built PzBefWg 35(t) and

PzBefWg 38(t). The exact distribution of Fu 8 long-range radios (as used in the SdKfz 267) and Fu 7 for ground-to-air communication (SdKfz 268) is unknown.

The lack of armoured command tanks equipped with long-range radios could be addressed by using soft-skinned vehicles fitted with the same equipment. Many problems stemmed from inadequate production: This would continue to trouble the military planners responsible for the Panzer divisions until the war ended. As a result the authorities were forced to improvise, but the situation would be exacerbated as combat losses mounted.

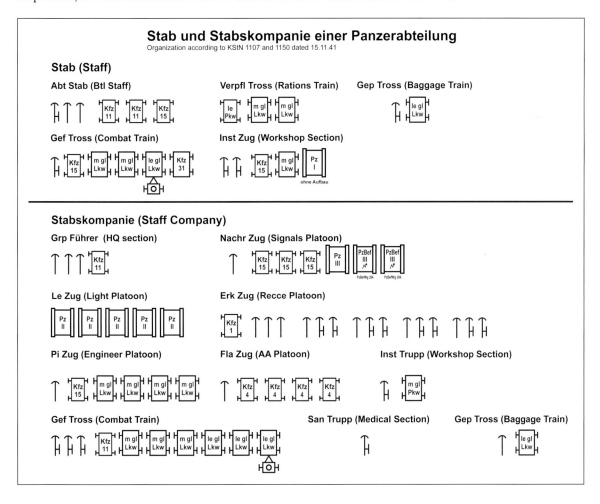

Panzerdivision as of 1940 – Provision of Signals Elements with Radios: Interoperability

1.PzDiv	2.PzDiv	3.PzDiv	4.PzDiv	5.PzDiv	6.PzDiv	7.PzDiv	8.PzDiv	9.PzDiv	10.PzDiv
8	16	27	10	25	14	8	15	12	18

Left:
A number of German tanks
from 3.PzDiv, including a kl
PzBefWg, some PzKpfw II
light tanks and a number
of PzKpfw III medium tanks,
spaced out across a field of
growing cereals.

CHAPTER 4

RIFLE BRIGADE

The second most important element in a Panzer division was the *Schützen* (motorized rifle infantry). German military planners were confident that the tank was fully capable of fulfilling its mission to break through front-line positions. They were also aware that after a tank division had penetrated enemy territory, infantry would be required to clear the enemy forces from and consolidate the territory gained, thus allowing the tank force to continue its rapid advance to further tactical success. The tank was not designed, neither were tactics developed, to engage in close combat with dug-in enemy infantry.

Military planners also concluded that for rifle units in a tank division to be an effective integral element, the force would have to be motorized: foot infantry could only march at approximately 4kph. Obviously, this was far too slow to keep up with a rapidly advancing tank attack. A number of soft-skinned vehicles were available, and the six-wheeled truck was chosen despite the type having poor cross-country performance. Better mobility had to be found.

The economic situation and poor production performance of German industry forced military planners to look for a simple solution. Cheap to produce and being built in large numbers, the motorcycle was chosen and ordered for the newly established *Kradschützen Battailon* (motorcycle rifle battalions).

On the battlefield, the tank force would call for infantry assistance when faced by a difficult combat situation. Also essential to the completion of a successful assault were the support forces: pioneers (field engineers) to

Far left:
The SdKfz 251/1 *Schützenpanzer*, also referred to as *Panzergrenadierwagen*, was the most valuable asset in the inventory of a *Schützenregiment*. Armoured protection and mobility on the battleground was essential for keeping casualties in the infantry to a minimum. Note a *Raketenpanzerbüchse* (RPzB – rocket-powered anti-tank rifle) 54 – known to troops as the *Panzerschreck* (tank fright) – is carried on the side of the vehicle.

Above:
The SdKfz 263, *schwerer Panzerfunkwagen* (s PzFuWg – heavy armoured radio car) was fitted with long-range radio equipment. The type was in production until 1943, and many remained in service until end of the war.

clear obstacles and mines and medical troops to recover the wounded. But these troops were extremely vulnerable to infantry fire and shrapnel from shells fired by enemy artillery. French troops were equipped with a type of armoured carrier which influenced the German military to equip their infantry with a similar type of vehicle.

In 1940, the rifle element of a German tank division was to be organized on similar lines to the tank element, but this was never achieved. In May 1940, 1.PzDiv, 2.PzDiv, 3.PzDiv, 6.PzDiv and 8.PzDiv had a rifle brigade formed with a rifle regiment with three rifle battalions and a motorcycle-mounted battalion. At the same time, 4.PzDiv, 5.PzDiv, 7.PzDiv, 9.PzDiv and 10.PzDiv had a rifle brigade formed as two rifle regiments, each with two rifle battalions. These divisions had to be content with smaller contingents of motorcycle-mounted units; usually one company for each battalion.

In January 1941, most tank divisions were reformed to have a rifle brigade comprising two regiments each with four battalions. There was also a motorcycle-mounted battalion.

In 1940, the number of *mittlerer gepanzerter Mannschaftstransportwagen* (medium armoured personnel carrier – SdKfz 251) required for front-line forces was barely realized. Only 1.PzDiv had 140 of these useful and efficient vehicles to equip all seven of its rifle companies. The other nine tank divisions had only one company equipped with the SdKfz 251; some 15 to 20 vehicles.

Brigade staff

The staff of the rifle brigade was organized according to KStN 54, dated 1 October 1937, and manned by three officers, three NCOs and 11 conscripts.

By mid-1940, this relatively small staff section was provided with an effective signals attachment. The section was also equipped with a number of motor vehicles and was issued with an armoured vehicle, usually an SdKfz 247 Ausf A or the SdKfz 247 Ausf B armoured command car. However, documentation shows that the brigade commander of 6.PzDiv was supplied with an SdKfz 266 *Panzerbefehlswagen* (command tank); possibly due to the poor cross-country performance of the SdKfz 247.

The signals platoon was formed as four *kleine Funktrupp* 'd' (kl FuTrp – light radio sections) each supplied with four radio-equipped SdKfz 261,

Below:
The SdKfz 261, *kleiner Panzerfunkwagen* (kl PzFuWg – light armoured radio car) carried the light radio section 'd' (mot), which was responsible for long-range communications in the headquarters (HQ) section of a Panzer division. Using the frame-type antenna the 30W S transmitter had a range of up to 50km (Morse) and 15km (voice). When an 8m telescopic mast was fitted, range increased to 150km (Morse) and 45km (voice).

Left:
Kradschützen (motorcycle-mounted infantry) were a vital asset in each Panzer division. Their highly mobile motorcycle combinations carried men and their weapons, even a light mortar and heavy machine guns. From 1942, the combinations were gradually replaced by the SdKfz 250 armoured half-track or the VW *Typ* 166 *Schwimmwagen*. (SZ photo)

light armoured cars. Two further *mittlere Funktrupp* (m FuTrp – medium radio sections) were issued with radio-equipped SdKfz 263 *Achtrad* (eight-wheel) heavy armoured cars. Also there were two cable telephone sections and a small number of supply vehicles.

Regiment staff

The two rifle regimental staffs in a Panzer division were organized according KStN 1104, dated 1 October 1937, and manned by three officers, three NCOs and eleven conscripts. The HQ section was equipped with two heavy cross-country cars and a number of motorcycles. A document from 6.PzDiv shows that the commanding officer commandeered a civilian sedan car for his personal use. A regimental staff company was formed according KStN 1153 and supported the staff and HQ sections. There was also a motorcycle-mounted platoon, a signals section and an engineer platoon.

Rifle battalion staff

The *Stab eines Schützen Battailons* (rifle battalion staff) was organized according two different organizational tables – both dated 1 November 1937 – KStN 1108 for units without an armoured rifle element, and KStN 1108 (gp) for units equipped with armoured personnel carriers. However, despite being fully equipped with the type, according to a dedicated KStN dated 26 October 1940, 1.PzDiv noted that KStN 1108 was the valid

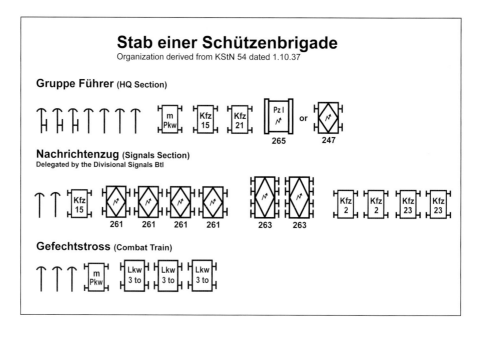

Stab eines Schützenregiments

Organization derived from KStN 1104 dated 1.10.37

Gruppe Führer (HQ Section)

Gefechtstross (Combat Train)

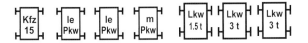

Verpflegungs- und Gefechtstross (Rations and Combat Train)

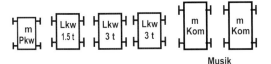

Musik

Below:
The SdKfz 247 was built in two versions. The Ausf A was basically an armoured version of the Krupp Protze of which 10 were produced. The type was not fitted with radio equipment and was not armed. The SdKfz 247 Ausf B was a purpose-built armoured command car.

Above:
Kradschützen (motorcycle-mounted infantry) troops were totally exposed to all weather – even the sidecar offered little protection. In 1941 when fighting in Russia, the winter temperature often fell to minus 40°C; many units were immobilized and a number were annihilated.

Right:
An SdKfz 261, possibly from 216.InfDiv during the advance into Russia. When on the march, with the frame-type antenna erected, the voice range of the 30W S radio was reduced to 10km.

structure. The exact date of the introduction of the 'armoured' staff remains unknown. A structure using KStN 1108 (gp), dated March 1942, indicates that 23.PzDiv had only one of two battalions in the rifle regiment as being armoured. It appears most probable that KStN 1108 was the only table being adhered to in 1940.

The HQ section was equipped with a number of motorcycles and three Kfz 15. The signals section was supplied with four radio or telephone-equipped cross-country cars. Two *kleine Funktrupp* 'd', light armoured radio sections, were issued with the SdKfz 261. Finally the supply section was issued with light, medium and heavy trucks and the workshop section had similar vehicles.

Stab eines Schützenbataillons
Organization derived from KStN 1108 dated 1.10.37

Gruppe Führer (HQ Section)

Nachrichtstaffel (Signals Section)

Gefechtstross (Combat Train)

Instandsetzungsstaffel (Workshop Section)   **Waffenmeisterei** (Armoury)

Verpflegungs- und Gefechtstross (Rations and Combat Train)

Left:
April 1938, with the Brandenburg Gate as a backdrop: An *Aufklärungs-Kompanie* (mot) (motorized reconnaissance company) parades for the benefit of the citizens of Berlin. The unit is led by an SdKfz 247 Ausf B and is followed by an SdKfz 232 (*sechsrad* – six wheeled [6 Rad]) radio car. The vehicles are painted in a pre-war camouflage scheme: dark brown stripes over dark grey.

Combat report from 8.Abt/PzRgt 1, dated 24 May 1940

Mission:

One platoon of 4.*Kompanie* (Kp – company), attached to 8.Kp is ordered to support riflemen as they attempt to widen to widen the bridgehead. A reconnaissance will be conducted during soon after dawn by *Leutnant* von Villebois and *Leutnant* Lucas.

Execution:

The first stream, which was reached the day before, is being crossed without any problems. The tanks give the riflemen fire support to help them on their approach to the second stream. Then they advance further to the next stream to provide further support during the crossing and to enlarge the bridgehead. Initially the attack progresses well, but is halted when the riflemen try to cross the stream in inflatable dinghies. The supporting PzKpfw IV began firing at houses: French troops have set up machine gun positions inside a number. The tanks fire high-explosive (HE) rounds with a delay fuse; a very effective way of destroying houses. The Panzer IV accomplished their mission successfully and began to operate in close cooperation with the riflemen which allowed them to widen the bridgehead without losses.

Below:
Commanders of the *Panzerwaffe* considered that a *Panzerbefehlswagen* (PzBefwg – command tank) was an important battlefield asset. The type, designated SdKfz 267, was based on the PzKpfw III, but was fitted with dedicated radio equipment. The type mounted a dummy main gun and a single *Maschinengewehr* (MG – machine gun) 34. This Sdkfz 267 is in service with PzRg 1.

The following report shows that close cooperation between the subunits in a Panzer division was absolutely necessary for a successful advance. But a tank can be halted by a barrier placed to block a road or mines, buried by the defending forces, and soon becomes an easy target for troops armed with anti-tank weapons. In such a situation *Panzerpionier* [field engineers] are ordered into action to clear any obstacle; a highly dangerous duty.

Combat report *Panzerpionier-Bataillon* 37 dated 10 June 1940

The battalion advances as the attack moves forward. The staff section relocates from Écly via Chateau Porcien to a wooded area southeast of Avancon and near the divisional HQ. On arrival the area is bombed by enemy aircraft.

Meanwhile, 1.Kp advances on Taizy, where the enemy is still putting up a dogged defence. After their arrival at 06.00hrs, 1.Kp is ordered to clear the road of obstacles and barriers and prepare for the advance. By 10.00hrs, the company commander reports to the *Schützenbrigade* leader that all obstacles had been removed. At 13.30hrs, 1.Kp is ordered to join III.Abt/SchRgt 1 as they begin to advance in the face of fierce enemy

Left:
German recovery units were equipped with the SdKfz 9, heavy half-track tractor to haul trailer units. The *Sonderanhänger* (SdAnh – special purpose trailer) 116 had a load-carrying capacity of some 22,350kg; sufficient for transporting tanks and assault guns in service during 1941.

Above:
Originally the PzKpfw IV
Ausf A, armed with a 7.5cm
KwK L/24, was designed
as a support tank and
consequently built with
relatively thin (14.5mm)
armour. But this was soon
found to be inadequate and
all subsequent models were
fabricated using thicker
armour plates.

resistance. At around 21.00hrs, we are attacked by a significant number of enemy tanks, but they are forced to halt and then retreat. Our troops dig-in for the night.

In the early hours of dawn, a tank attack is launched with 1.Kp following the last wave. Within a short time, the lead tank penetrates the enemy's front-line positions, but then is halted by accurate fire from enemy anti-tank guns and tanks. Following immediately behind our tanks are the men of 4.Zug (platoon) transported in SdKfz 251, armoured half-track vehicles. [Records kept by the tank regiment, indicate that this was the first time armoured half-tracks were used in conjunction with a tank assault.] At first the battalion was unsure about this deployment, but soon realized the benefits of having armoured pioneers integrated in the front-line force.

On reaching the river Retourne, which flows across the northern boundary of Neuflize, our attack is halted: the enemy has erected more obstacles to block the roads, laid mines and demolished all the bridges. The men of III.Abt/SchRgt 1 become detached during the assault, which forces brigade HQ to order 1.*Pionier-Kompanie* to clear the obstacles and attack Neuflize. To assist the company to achieve its task the unit was reinforced by a platoon of Panzer IV from II.Abt/PzRgt 1. The task confronting the troops is dangerous, since the enemy has established a number of defensive positions in houses, barns and even the village church and is firing through windows and from roof hatches. Under cover of fire from our tanks, 4.Zug approaches to within 200m of the enemy positions. Now the pioneer sections dismount from the vehicles and advance toward the first obstacle, while the attached tanks provide effective fire support. The platoon commander and his pioneers advance to the barrier behind a PzKpfw II which not only offers some protection but also provides covering fire to allow the troops to achieve their task of removing all the obstacles and mines. The mission is accomplished in a short time, but during the action one pioneer is fatally wounded. Now the tanks of the company and the attached PzKpfw IV platoon use the opportunity to advance. Pioneers armed with hand grenades, follow close behind each tank. The enemy is quickly cleared from one building after another.

Due to the action of the pioneer company, it took a mere 30 minutes to capture Neuflize and begin preparations to cross the main river. Interestingly, the tank company ran out of fuel and was forced to wait until 21.00hrs to be replenished. Finally, the battle had shown that armoured pioneers were a vital asset to a successful attack by armoured forces.

Below:
During the invasion of France, the tank crews of PzRgt 1 were alarmed to discover that the armour of the PzKpfw III could be easily penetrated at close range; even by fire from a light anti-tank gun. As an expedient, many crews fitted spare track links on the superstructure to improve protection, a practice that became widely used during the war.

Combat report Panzer-Brigade 1 of 1.PzDiv, 10 June 1940

At 06.30hrs, the attack by the Panzer-Brigade commences in southern direction, the infantry of 17.InfDiv follow in close support. Enemy resistance is very weak allowing our advance to proceed at an unexpectedly fast pace; the open terrain between villages provides little cover for the defenders. Our tanks make the breakthrough and 17.InfDiv exploits the attack in the best way allowing rapid progress to be made.

At 08.34hrs, I./PzRgt 1 crossed the road leading from Tagnon to Neuflize. At 09.00hrs, the forces of PzRgt 1 reach the river Retourne [a tributary of the Aisne], but our advance is halted due to a surrounding area of marshland. Now our 7.5cm-armed PzKpfw IV open fire on enemy artillery positions and also to attack, with much success, French troop movements to the southwest of Neuflize. This is possible due to our special aiming device [a calibrated plate mounted on the *Turmzielfernrohr* (TZF – turret sighting telescope)] which increases effective accuracy to 4,000m.

After crossing the road, with a number of PzKpfw III from PzRgt 2 guarding our eastern flank, the advance on Alincourt began. On reaching the village we found that the southern bank of the Retourne was held by the enemy. A number of enemy engineers had

Below:
The crew of this PzKpfw III Ausf E has decided to considerably improve armour protection by welding small strips of plate to vulnerable areas, including above the driver's vision slit. Note that the crew has utilized the driver's hatches taken from destroyed French H-35 tanks.

Above:
A German signals unit during preparations for the attack on Poland in 1939. The lead vehicle is a Horch 840, followed by two Büssing NAG G31 fitted with box-type bodies typically used by administration personnel.

been captured and after interrogation it was concluded that the approaches to Alincourt had been heavily mined. A ford in the river, near the village, can only be crossed by PzKpfw III and PzKpfw IV, it being too deep for our PzKpfw I and PzKpfw II. During the fighting in the vicinity of the village, our forces captured a French heavy artillery battery.

The only alternative route by which to cross the river is the bridge at Neuflize; here 2./PzPiBtl 37 begins the task of removing demolition charges placed by French engineers, but is met with determined enemy resistance. Immediately, PzRgt 1 is called up to provide covering fire for our engineers working to defuse the mines.

At 11.53hrs, II/PzRgt 1 crossed the bridge and as it began to enter the captured village the enemy suddenly launched a tank counterattack from the south, but this was easily repelled. The Brigadeführer (brigade commander) has given orders for an advance further toward Juniville by keeping close to the river before turning south and out of the range of French artillery. A worrying problem: the wooded area to the south of our advance conceals French artillery positions from which we expect heavy fire. With this knowledge, the crews of our advancing tanks have become very nervous and begin to blanket the area with ferocious but haphazard fire. Alarmed by their action, the Brigadeführer orders the advance to be halted and the tanks withdrawn. He then orders all crews to assemble where he orders them to observe strict fire discipline and not waste ammunition.

The attack resumes and our forces advance to 3km south of Juniville; here PzRgt 1 is engaged by a number of French tanks (Char B1bis). A fierce firefight began as the tanks of PzRgt 1 and PzRgt 2 engage the enemy; a long fight ensued until the amount of ammunition consumed reached an alarming level and forced our tanks to retreat for replenishment. But the enemy exploited this short pause in the fighting, and continued with sporadic fire from individual tanks. This action, however, has proven that our armour-piercing weapons and ammunition is ineffective against these heavily armoured tanks.

The *Brigadeführer* – Oberst Krüger – orders an armoured reconnaissance unit to cross open fields toward the occupied woods, but it is attacked by well-concealed French anti-tank guns and almost wiped out. Although an urgent signal requesting artillery support was sent, our guns remained silent. The tank force commanded by Balck, which was advancing from the north, had been delayed by the fighting en-route but was still expected soon. A discussion between Krüger and the regiment commanders saw them agree that it is necessary to wait and use the time to regroup and replenish. When Krüger met with Balck, *Generaloberst* Guderian made an unexpected appearance and during their impromptu meeting the three officers agreed that an immediate attack was

Right:
Engineers from PzRgt 1 have erected a field workshop at the edge of a wood. The large camouflaged tents not only protected the men and vehicles from the weather, but also from enemy reconnaissance or bomber aircraft. Such facilities were usually erected a safe distance from the frontline.

required. Unfortunately the PzKpfw IV tanks, deemed essential, will not be available due to a shortage of ammunition and a number of mechanical problems.

The decision is taken to clear enemy forces from woodland south of Juniville, and III.Abt/SchtzRgt 1 is selected to lead the attack supported by a platoon of PzKpfw II [eight tanks] from each regiment to provide covering fire. At the same time, the tank brigade is to push further south through Neuville-en-Tournay and establish a bridgehead at Bétheniville. After an artillery bombardment, the attack by III.Abt/SchtzRgt supported by 6./PzRgt 2 begins at 21.00hrs, but the assault is halted and our troops retreat. The regiments take up new positions in a 'hedgehog' formation for the night and establish a brigade command post. A fresh attack is planned for the next day, but this time supported with the extra firepower of 4./PzRgt 2 and a heavy FlaK platoon to ensure that the enemy is defeated.

The tank regiments were dependent on the assistance of other subunits, as it applied vice versa. A combat report shows the value of the PzKpfw IV armed with a short-barrelled 7.5cm KwK L/24 in assisting attacking riflemen.

CHAPTER 5

COMBAT ELEMENTS

A lthough the tank and infantry elements were the main combat units in a Panzer division it could not operate effectively without a large number of attached units. Indeed the support and supply services outnumbered the fighting force.

German military doctrine saw that the men in all subunits were, if required, to fight alongside the main combat elements. For instance, a field cook was issued with a rifle and was expected to fight with the infantry or shoot at low-flying enemy aircraft. An NCO from the supply section would be expected to join anti-tank troops attacking tanks which had broken through the defences.

Between 1925 and 1935, Guderian had elaborated his plans for the *Panzertruppe*. With the benefit of hindsight, the many essays and books he published appear to be theoretical and somewhat overly sophisticated. However, a careful study of his works would reveal to a reader the true value of his thoughts (see *Die Panzertruppen* by Heinz Guderian). Firstly he defined the two main elements, *Aufklärungskörper* (reconnaissance corps) which he saw as being vitally important and the *Schlachtkörper* (combat corps). In further pages he went on to describe in detail almost all the elements of what would become a Panzer division.

Subsequently, his ideas were taken up and used as the basis for the manual D 66+ (dated December 1940), which explained the tasks of a Panzer division.

This very basic manual also emphasized the importance of reconnaissance, since it would be these units which should, in most instances, be the first to come into contact with the enemy.

Far left:
In 1942, the PzKpfw IV was upgraded by installing the 7.5cm KwK 40 L/43 long-barrelled gun and over the following year it became the most important German battle tank. This photograph, taken in France after the D-Day landings on 6 June 1944, is of a PzKpfw IV Ausf H from 2.PzDiv which has received a Zimmerit coating and is fitted with *Panzerschürzen* (side skirts). Note an MG 34 has been fitted in the anti-aircraft mounting.

Right:
The PzKpfw III Ausf E, armed with a 3.7cm KwK L/45, was deployed for the invasion of Poland and later *Fall Gelb* (Plan Yellow); the invasion of France. At that time the gun was considered to be sufficiently powerful, but tank crews soon demanded a better weapon.

Left:
In December 1941 an improved version of the PzKpfw III mounting a 5cm KwK L/60 gun, designated Ausf J, entered service. All the crewmen are wearing camouflage smocks rather than the conventional *Sonderbekleidung für Panzerbesatzungen* (tanker's uniform).

Left:
A line of tanks being prepared prior to the launch of *Unternehmen Zitadelle* (Operation *Citadel*) in mid-1943; the second vehicle is a PzKpfw IV *Flammpanzer* (flamethrower tank).

Above:
A new PzKpfw III Ausf L loaded on a railway wagon for delivery to a Panzer division; note the 5cm KwK L/60 gun appears to be wrapped with oiled paper for protection. A number of improvements began to be fitted: a 20mm armour plate was fitted to the front plate of the superstructure and a protective plate for the gun mantlet. However, due to ever-present material shortages not all could be modified. Note this tank has the extra armour, but no plate over the mantlet.

The main fighting element in a Panzer division was the tank force – organized in company, battalion or regiment strength – which would form the spearhead of any attack.

Although the tank was the essential part of the Panzer division, it could not be deployed without the support of other weapons and in close cooperation with all units.

The *schützen* (rifle infantry) brigade would lead an attack where the terrain was not suitable for the commitment of tanks, or where enemy forces had built obstacles or laid mines. Another reason was that the *schützen* were highly mobile and could cross the battlefield at great speed. As the war progressed, the infantry would be equipped with the *Schützenpanzerwagen* (SPw – armoured troop carrier), which made it possible for them to keep pace with the tanks. In combat it was standard (pre-war) practice for the troops to dismount and fight, but later in the war, they were allowed to remain inside their vehicle and continue to fight.

From the beginning, the guns of the artillery were to be towed by motor vehicles allowing these units to keep pace with the advancing Panzer division. The batteries would also have to be highly manoeuvrable and always on the alert to provide effective fire support when called on.

The *Panzerjäger* (anti-tank element) had not only to fight and destroy enemy tanks, but also to supply defensive fire when required. Often they would be called on to neutralize enemy anti-tank guns or machine-gun nests in support of the infantry.

The *Panzerpioniere* (armoured engineers) would closely follow the tank force during an attack and be ready to perform a number of duties.

- Clearing obstacles, barriers and mines while under fire on the battlefield.
- Reconnaissance of minefields and clearing safe pathways.
- Construction of bridges in accordance with weight requirements.

The *Panzernachrichten-Abteilung* (tank signals battalion) provided radio and cable telephone services; reliable communication was a basic requirement for a fast-moving Panzer division. Different types of radio equipment were supplied which worked on various wavelengths allowing short or long-range contact in voice or Morse code.

The *leichte Flugzeugabwehrkanone Abteilung* (le FlaKAbt – light anti-aircraft battalion) provided the important anti-aircraft protection. However, the divisional staff did not issue this subunit with sufficient guns to provide protection for an entire division.

Below:
Steering brake failure (note the open maintenance hatches) has brought this PzKpfw IV Ausf B from 2.PzDiv to a halt in a French town. The crew has named the tank 'Elfriede'.

The reconnaissance battalion

The *Aufklärungs-Abteilung* (mot) was a vital part of the division.

During the establishment of the first German armoured formations, Guderian became aware of how important effective *Aufklärungs* (reconnaissance) would be for a highly mobile Panzer division. As a result he demanded the formation of a significant number of well-equipped (reconnaissance) motorized units to attached to the tank forces.

German intelligence units classified information as follows:

Strategische aufklärung (strategic reconnaissance) served to gather general information on hostile nations; in particular their military. Much of this was garnered from articles in newspapers, newsreels in cinemas, contact with politicians and diplomats. German military attachés were often invited to witness military manoeuvres and visit armaments factories. Also, Germany would have had network of spies in each country.

Operative aufklärung (operational reconnaissance) supplied information for those in the higher echelons of military command planning battlefield strategy. Most of this type of reconnaissance was normally conducted by the *Luftwaffe* flying photographic missions.

Taktische aufklärung (tactical reconnaissance) on the battlefield was provided by the subunits attached to a Panzer division. The units, often operating far ahead of the battlefront, provided a survey of the terrain, observed enemy positions and attempted to identify the class of troops involved; vital information before the commitment of an assault force.

Far left:
Two versions of the *kleiner Panzefunkwagen* (kl PzFuWg – light armoured radio car) were produced: the SdKfz 261 fitted a frame-type antenna and was equipped with an Fu 8 radio, and the SdKfz 260 (shown) mounted a 2m rod-type aerial and an Fu 7 radio for air-to-ground communication with *Luftwaffe* aircraft.

Left:
An SdKfz 221, *leichte Panzerspähwagen* (le PzSpWg – light armoured car), was used to equip the *Aufklärungs-Abteilung* (mot) (AufklKp – reconnaissance company [motorized]) of a Panzer division. The lightly armed (MG 34) type was not originally fitted with radio equipment, but this lack was remedied in 1941.

Left:
A column of motor vehicles from *Panzergruppe* 3; the stylized 'h', identifies that the group was commanded by General Hermann Hoth. Note the French-built Panhard 178 – *Panzerspähwagen* 204(f) – armoured car; some 190 of these vehicles were captured and subsequently used by a number of German units. Note the vehicle is fitted with a frame antenna.

In the first months of World War II, German military planners became more focused on the value of battlefield reconnaissance and ordered the establishment of a battalion-size motorized unit in the Panzer division: an original proposal by Guderian.

In 1940, the establishment of the *Aufklarungs-Abteilung* (mot) (AufKlAbt – reconnaissance battalion [motorized]) of the *Panzertruppe* was not achieved with any uniformity, since the armoured cars were issued somewhat randomly. Any shortfall was made up by deploying the highly mobile *Kradschützen* (KradSchtz – motorcycle infantry).

In mid-1941, the designation *Aufklärungs-Abteilung* (mot) was changed to *Panzer-Aufklärungs-Abteilung* (PzAufKlAbt – armoured reconnaissance battalion), emphasizing the combat principles of the Panzer division. Parallel to this development, the AufKlAbt (mot) establishment was considerably improved. During the invasion of Russia it became obvious that the *Kradschützen* had met the limits of their tactical use. In 1942, all AufKlAbt were issued armoured half-tracks (SdKfz 250 and 251) and also four-wheeled and eight-wheeled armoured vehicles.

Although organizational structures for the AufKlAbt (mot) were issued promptly, the provision of reconnaissance units attached to the Panzer divisions was not uniform. Some 20 Panzer divisions and a number of SS units received French-built Panhard P178 armoured cars captured after the invasion of France.

Right:
In July 1942, the first *schwere Panzerspähwagen* (s PzSpWg – heavy armoured car) entered service. The type utilized the chassis and superstructure of the *Achtrad* (eight wheeled) and mounted a 7.5cm KwK L/24; it was designated SdKfz 233. The vehicle was issued to armoured reconnaissance companies.

Staff

The *Stab einer Aufklärungs-Abteilung* (staff of the reconnaissance battalion was organized according to KStN 1105. The commander was issued with an SdKfz 247 Ausf B, and the unit had two motorcycles and two Kfz 15.

Note: The SdKfz 247 was built in small numbers. The Ausf A was an armoured version of the Krupp-built Kfz 69, also known as the Protze: 10 were built. A total of 58 SdKfz 247 Ausf B, armoured command car, were built by Daimler-Benz on the chassis of a Horch 108. Normally these vehicles were not fitted with a weapon or radio equipment, but it is most likely that some front-line units did fit these items. Some survived until the raid to Stalingrad.

The staff train was provided with a combination, several medium cars, six light trucks and an Kfz 31 ambulance.

Above:
The VW *Typ* 166, better known as the *Schwimmwagen*, was developed alongside the *Kübelwagen* as a replacement for the motorcycle combinations used by *Kradschützen* (motorcycle infantry) units. The type, cheaper to produce than a combination, had far superior off-road mobility, better load-carrying capacity and could cross water obstacles.

Right:
After mass production of the SdKfz 250 had begun, *Inspektion* (In – inspector) 6 ordered the development of a 2cm KwK 38 L/55-armed armoured reconnaissance variant. The type was to utilize the same turret as the SdKfz 222 and be ready for service by March 1942. The vehicle was designated SdKfz 250/9.

Signals staff

The *Stab Nachrichten-Zug einer Aufklärungs-Abteilung* (staff section of the signals platoon in a reconnaissance battalion), to KStN 1191, was issued with three motorcycles, a Kfz 15 and a light truck.

Ten radio sections formed the core of the battalion. Four *mittlerer Funktrupp* (m FuTrp – medium radio sections) 'b', equipped with the 100W transmitter and two Torn E 'b' portable receivers, provided long-range radio communications. Two were issued with Kfz 15 and Kfz 17 cross-country cars; two *mittlere Panzer-Funktrupp (gepanzert)* (m PzFuTrp [gp] – medium tank radio section [armoured]) were equipped with the SdKfz 263 and a Kfz 15. When transmissions were made using a telescopic mast, a voice range of 70km (200km Morse) was achievable. When transmitting using the frame-type antenna it was possible to achieve a voice range of 20km (80km Morse). During the march, using vehicle-mounted aerials, a voice range of 10km (50km Morse) was achievable.

Four *kleine Panzer-Funktrupp* (kl PzFuTrp – light tank radio section) 'd' were equipped with the SdKfz 261 fitted with a 30W S 'a' transmitter with a voice range of 50km (150km Morse) using a telescopic mast and 15km (50km Morse) using the frame-type antenna. A Torn E 'b' portable receiver was also carried in the vehicle.

One kl PzFuTrp was issued with an SdKfz 260 fitted with a 20W S 'a' transmitter which had a voice range of 50km using the 2m rod antenna.

Also, a Torn E 'b' portable receiver was carried in the vehicle.

Two TornFuTrp 'b' (portable radio section) equipped with TornFuG 'b' were issued with Kfz 2 light cross-country cars.

The *kleine Fernsprechtrupp* (kl FernsprTrp – light telephone cable-layer section) 'c', was equipped with the Kfz 15 or Kfz 17 cross-country vehicles.

Armoured reconnaissance

The PzAufklAbt had two *Panzerspäh-Kompanie (armoured reconnaissance companies)*, organized according to KStN 1162. Each company had several subunits.

Headquarters

The most senior officer in the *Gruppe Führer* (company HQ) was supplied (when available) with an SdKfz 247 Ausf B. The HQ section was also issued with a Kfz 11, cross-country car, and twelve motorcycles for dispatch riders.

Below:
An artillery observation post in the North African desert: the aerial fitted on the SdKfz 221 indicates that the vehicle is fitted a Torn E 'b' portable receiver. Note the reconnaissance team has positioned a tripod-mounted *Scherenfernrohr* (scissors periscope) to assess range.

Left:
A number of late production
SdKfz 232 PzSpWg (Fu)
vehicles from an armoured
reconnaissance battalion
loaded on railway wagons
for transportation to the
frontline. In 1942, the
conspicuous frame-type
antennae began to be
replaced by the *Sterantenne*
(star antenna) 'd'.

Right:
Since there was a surplus of 7.5cm [KwK 37] L/24 guns it was decided to mount the type on the SdKfz 250 chassis by modifying the superstructure. Designated SdKfz 251/8, and often known as the *Kanonenwagen*, the vehicles were delivered to Panzer grenadier battalions.

Below:
A reconnaissance section consisting of three SdKfz 231 and an SdKfz 223) have reinforced their numbers by utilizing a South African-built Marmon Herrington armoured car captured from Allied forces. German units in North Africa were never supplied with sufficient equipment.

Signals

The *Nachrichtenstaffel* (signals section) consisted of an m PzFuTrp (gp) equipped with an SdKfz 263 and also a Kfz 15 cross-country vehicle. The unit also had four le PzSpWg (Fu) (SdKfz 223) at its disposal. These vehicles were fitted with the same radio as a kl FuTrp 'd': the Torn E 'b' receiver and 30W S transmitter had a voice range of 15km (50km Morse) when using a collapsible frame-type antenna.

Armoured reconnaissance (light)

Two elements of the *Aufklärungs-Abteilung* (AufklAbt – reconnaissance battalion) were the *leichte Panzerspäh-Zug* (le PzSpZg – light armoured reconnaissance platoon), but both had different equipment.

One le PzSpZg had a complement of six SdKfz 221 *leichter Panzerspähwagen Maschinengewehr* (le PzSpWg [MG] – light armoured car [machine gun]). In 1940, these light armoured vehicles were not fitted with radio equipment, but all were equipped with a FuSprech 'a' in preparation for *Unternehmen* (Operation) Barbarossa.

The other le PzSpZg was equipped with four le PzSpWg (MG), SdKfz 221 and four 2cm-armed le PzSpWg, SdKfz 222. As with the SdKfz 221, the SdKfz 222 had also not originally been equipped with radio.

Armoured reconnaissance (heavy)

One *schwerer Panzerspäh-Zug* (s PzSpZg – heavy armoured reconnaissance platoon) received six of the new *Achtrad* (eight-wheeled) heavy armoured car which had a far superior cross-country performance and range than the le PzSpWg.

Three were *schwere Panzerspähwagen* (s PzSpWg – heavy armoured car), SdKfz 231. All were armed with a 2cm KwK 30 cannon and an MG 34, but were not fitted with radio equipment.

The other three were the SdKfz 232 variant fitted with Fu 11 SE 100 long-range radio equipment: a 100W S transmitter linked to Torn E 'b' receiver as used by the m FuTrp 'b'.

The platoon also had a *Gefechtstross* (combat train) and *Gepäcktross* (baggage) train to carry equipment. This was supplied with three motorcycles, two Kfz 15 cross-country vehicles and ten light or medium trucks.

Motorcycle reconnaissance

The reconnaissance battalion was also issued with a *Kradschützen-Kompanie* (KradSchKp – motorcycle rifle company). The KradSchKp, organized according to KStN 1111 dated October 1937, being a highly mobile unit

Above:
The SdKfz 250, armoured half-track vehicle, had a much better mobility over soft and rough terrain than an SdKfz 222 wheel-driven armoured car. The SdKfz 250/9 was fitted with a short-range FuSpreGer 'f', and usually operated in company with an SdKfz 250/5 fitted with a long-range Fu 12. Each *Spähtrupp* (reconnaissance section) was issued with two SdKfz 250/9 and an SdKfz 250/5.

was used for both reconnaissance and also combat missions.

The *Kompanietrupp* (staff section) was equipped with two Kfz 11 and/or 15 cross-country cars and four motorcycles including two combinations (motorcycle with sidecar).

The company was formed as three *Kradschützen-Zug* (motor-cycle rifle platoon), each with two cross-country cars (Kfz 11 and/or 15) and three motorcycle sections, each with three combinations. Also there was a *Granatwerfer* (GrWrf – mortar) section with two combinations; one to carry the 5cm GrWrf 36.

A further *Maschinengewehr Halbzug* (MgH – machine-gun section) was equipped with ten combinations: two mounted with MG 34 machine guns.

The company *Gefechtstross and Gepäcktross* were issued with three motorcycles, two cross-country cars and six light trucks.

Heavy company

The *schwere Kompanie einer Aufklärungs-Abteilung* (s Kp – heavy company) had several *Teileinheiten* (TE – independent elements) attached to provide precious support services, including pioneers, anti-tank and field artillery also infantry.

The *Kompanietrupp* (staff section), was equipped, according to KStN 1121 dated October 1937, with a Kfz 15 cross-country car and four combinations. The unit also had a combat and baggage train, equipped with four combinations, two cross-country cars, six light trucks and a 3-ton truck.

The *Pionier-Zug* (mot) (PiZug – engineer platoon [motorized]) was formed according to KStN 1124, dated October 1937, had a complement of four motorcycles (including one combination), three Kfz 15 and five *Pionier-Kraftwagen* (trucks with engineer equipment). The PiZug also used *Flosssäcke* (inflatable dinghies) which were carried on a truck. Their bridging equipment was carried in two trucks.

The *Panzerjäger-Zug* (anti-tank platoon), according KStN 1122, the platoon leader was supplied with a Kfz 69 and the three 3.7cm PaK were towed by Kfz 69 (light gun tractors) supported by a Kfz 69 ammunition carrier. The unit also had two motorcycles for their dispatch riders.

Below:
Pioneer troops ferry a motorcycle combination over a stream. The *grosser Flosssäck* 34 (large inflatable dinghy) had a capacity of 1,250 kg, sufficient to carry seven men, or a 3.7cm PaK anti-tank gun or a motorcycle combination.

The *Infanteriegeschütz-Zug* (infantry gun platoon), according KStN 1123, was equipped with two 7.5cm *leichtes Infanterie-Geschütz* (leIG – light infantry gun) 18 towed the Kfz 69. Another Kfz 69 towed a *Sonderanhänger* (SdAnh – special-purpose trailer) 32 carrying ammunition. The platoon leader was supplied with a Kfz 12, three motorcycles (two were combinations). The platoon also had a *leichter Feldkabelbautrupp* (light telephone section) which used a Kfz 15.

Light transport train

The combat, rations and baggage trains used a number of cross-country cars and a large number of light, medium and heavy trucks. The column would be accompanied by a Kfz 31 *Krankenkraftwagen* (KrKw – ambulance). The engineer workshop section was issued with a number of trucks to carry tools, special machinery and lifting equipment. Despite the battalion having an allotment of armoured cars (including heavy types), no recovery vehicle such as a half-track tractor was issued.

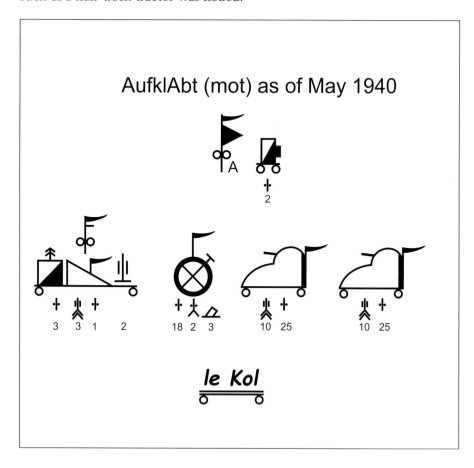

Note: A *schwere Kompanie* (s Kp – heavy company) was also attached to each rifle battalion and was equipped with the Kfz 69. The divisional *Panzerjäger-Abteilung* (PzJgAbt – anti-tank battalion) was supplied with the SdKfz 10 which had superior cross-country performance. Also *Teileinheiten* were part of other subunits in the division.

Depending on availability, it was possible that variations in the exact provision were common. For instance, if an SdKfz 260 or 261 radio-equipped armoured car was not available it was often replaced by a Kfz 17.

The following after-action report provides a good impression of a dramatic combat by an armoured personnel carrier-equipped company.

Anton Hänle, *Unteroffizier* [Uffz – Sergeant]
2./PzGrenRgt 304
In combat, 14 September 1942

Experience:
Counterattack using *Schützenpanzer* (SPw – armoured personnel carriers) during a Russian attack at Ryabinki:

9 August 1942. The sun has set in the west. A dispatch rider delivers the order to get ready. We [infantry soldiers], ask him what is the matter. He replies; "it stinks, Ivan is attacking through the dense woodland."

The platoon, all experienced *Landser* (troopers), quickly get ready. We leave our positions and dig new trenches some 600m further ahead. We all watch the edge of the woods very carefully. What will happen? We keep hidden in our new positions for several hours. Suddenly we hear the sound of engines approaching: Our *Schützenpanzer* have arrived.

The second battalion, which is positioned in front of us to the left, comes under fire. One of our young troopers remarks that something is going on in the woods. The machine gunners in the SPw ready their weapons. The order to advance is given and we follow the vehicles closely, and approach to within 200m of the wood. Suddenly the machine gunners open fire, followed by detonations of high-explosive (HE) rounds fired from our 3.7cm PaK [platoon leaders were issued with an SdKfz 251/103]. The Soviets respond, filling the air with bullets. The wood is full of enemy soldiers – a fierce fight starts. We see a muzzle blast from near a tree stump, possibly from an anti-tank rifle or gun. We cannot move without covering fire. We advance to the wood in short stages using every trough or furrow in the ground. Our PaK-armed SPw attacks a number of mortar positions and machine-gun nests with much success. Suddenly it stops and begins to emit smoke; it has been hit by an anti-tank rifle, but the crew escape from the vehicle. To avoid any further losses, all the other vehicles seek cover behind bushes. Some have also received hits, but are still operational.

Now the Russian concentrates fire on the dismounted *Panzergrenadiere* on the ground in front of the wood. Despite the noise of combat I can hear shouts for help. The squad commanded by Heiner Krause, advancing to the left of my position is hit and disperses under heavy enemy fire as it attempts to advance to the wood. Krasse is seriously wounded and my MG Schütze 1 (machine-gunner 1) tries to help him and leaps forward – falling back immediately, fatally wounded. A shell from an anti-tank rifle had ripped the barrel housing off his MG which then struck him. My other MG is firing hard at enemy positions, but is spotted by the enemy and targeted. The MG gunner is wounded and we recover him to a shallow depression. Here we find the rest of my squad, two No.2 MG gunners and a rifleman: too few to defend against the advancing enemy. At this moment our armoured carriers attack again, approaching from the right; immediately the enemy moves his fire and concentrates on our half-tracks. We cannot continue to advance; the Soviets are in well-concealed positions and every move we make is met with heavy fire. Also we are under continuous mortar fire. The half-track crews respond with machine-gun fire. Uffz Hübner throws one hand grenade after another from his vehicle, which kill or wound a number of enemy soldiers. But despite his success he is forced to retreat again. Now a number of the crews fall victim to hand grenades being tossed into their vehicles. We hear loud shouts calling for medics. The fight develops into close combat, machine guns 'chatter', mortar shells explode with a thump and bullets whine overhead – all hell has broken loose. Our armoured carriers are forced to retreat since the enemy is far too strong. We, too, must go back, but how? We must attempt to recover our weapons and ammunition. Sadly our dead and wounded will have to be left to the mercy of the Soviets.

Suddenly our artillery brings some salvation by laying a dense smoke screen to conceal us from the enemy. This allows us to begin our retreat through heavy mud sump and reed beds.

Under the cover of darkness, some armoured carriers are deployed to collect wounded for quick treatment. Where possible, the dead are also retrieved and taken to the cemetery.

We remain alert during the night expecting further attacks. The battlefront is silent since Soviet forces appear to be regrouping and remaining in their positions.

Our company has survived and despite suffering heavy casualties we feel proud that one company was able to stop and defeat an entire enemy battalion.

The report reveals the advantages of a modern armoured force such as a Panzer division. The slogan, '*Schützenpanzer sparen Blut*' – armoured personnel carriers save blood. The fundamental idea to provide the *Schützen* (renamed *Panzergrenadiere*) with these versatile vehicles proved to be right.

Vehicles such as the SdKfz 250 and SdKfz 251 carried a wide variety of weapons, including machine guns, a light anti-tank gun, an infantry mortar, and even a flamethrower. The armoured vehicle allowed men and weapons to advance close to enemy positions, often to devastating effect, since the type could move independently and unhindered. Using the benefits of mobility and speed, an enemy line could be penetrated and then attacked from the rear. In a difficult situation an equally rapid retreat was possible, keeping one's own personnel losses low. Although Germany was the first to introduce and use this type of vehicle in combat, a lack of industrial capacity made it almost impossible to produce the required number of these vital vehicles.

The Soviets sought and found ways of slowing down or stopping an attack led by armoured half-tracks by using anti-tank guns or their feared anti-tank rifle. As shown in this report, German formations often encountered numerically superior Soviet formations

Finally, the report (although written by a German soldier) shows that a German rifle company was capable of withstanding an attack by a much stronger enemy force. This correlation of forces was more or less the rule on the Eastern Front. Numerous reports underline a horrific disproportion between German and Russian losses.

Below:
The SdKfz 251 not only had excellent road and cross-country performance, but also armoured protection for the *Schützen* (riflemen) it carried. The type mounted two MG 34 machine guns which could be fired from inside the vehicle. To provide extra protection – the armour could be penetrated by infantry armour-piercing ammunition – the crew has mounted track links to the front.

Right:
In November 1942, the first SdKfz 233 vehicles to be delivered were issued to PzRgt 7 of 10.PzDiv, which at that time was deployed in North Africa. The 7.5cm KwK 37 L/24 was an effective weapon which gave reconnaissance units the ability to provide long-range fire support.

ARMOURED ELEMENTS

In 1940, before the invasion of France, the *Panzerwaffe* had begun to implement a number of changes. Guderian had planned for five Panzer divisions to be combat ready by 1940. Each would be formed as a Panzer brigade, two Panzer regiments, and four Panzer battalions. Overall, each division was to have eight light tank companies and four heavy companies.

To achieve the ultimate combat efficiency, the military planners decided to issue each light company with 23 PzKpfw III armed with a 3.7cm KwK L/45. Each heavy company was to have 15 PzKpfw IV escort tanks armed with a 7.5cm KwK L/24.

However, it was not feasible for that number of tanks to be delivered due to production problems in the Reich. To make up any shortfall, planners were forced to deploy PzKpfw I and PzKpfw II light tanks. Problems in delivering even a reduced number of tanks led to much confusion within the divisions. In 1938, possibly due to equipment supply problems, the number of tank companies was reduced to two light and one heavy in each battalion.

For administrative and logistic duties, each battalion had a *leichte Kolonne* (leKol – light column) and a *Staffel* (replacement platoon). The le Kol (PzAbt) was a platoon-sized unit providing transport services to the staff company in the battalion. The *Staffel* held a number of tanks in reserve

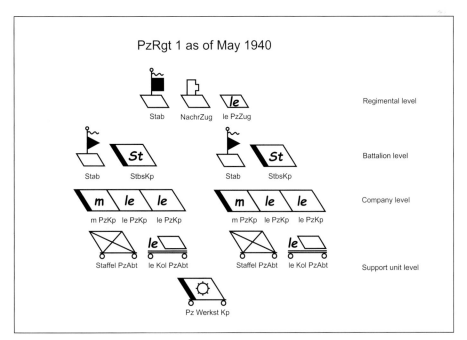

PzRgt 1 as of May 1940

| | | | Regimental level |
| Stab | NachrZug | le PzZug | |

| | | Battalion level |
| Stab | StbsKp | Stab | StbsKp |

| | | | Company level |
| m PzKp | le PzKp | le PzKp | m PzKp | le PzKp | le PzKp |

| | | | Support unit level |
| Staffel PzAbt | le Kol PzAbt | Staffel PzAbt | le Kol PzAbt |

Pz Werkst Kp

Far left:
A PzKpfw IV Ausf H from 2.PzDiv fitted with *Panzerschürzen* (side skirts); the 5mm-thick plates were fitted as extra protection for the thin armour on the hull sides against anti-tank rifle fire. But the mounting brackets were inadequate and individual plates became easily detached.

ready to replace any combat losses. In the authorized structure KStN 1178, dated 1 October 1938, the *Staffel* should have a reserve of one PzKpfw IV, one PzKpfw III, two PzKpfw II and three PzKpfw I. The unit was later disbanded and its role taken over by a divisional reserve company.

The Panzer regiment had a *Werkstattkompanie* (workshop company) responsible for establishing a field workshop to carry out maintenance and repairs for both tank battalions. The unit also had several mobile repair sections which undertook the hazardous task of repairing damaged tanks in the field. The workshop company also had a recovery squad which removed immobilized tanks, often from the battlefront, and transported them back to the workshop.

However, despite the omnipresent problem of supply, new and very optimistic KStN were published in 1939.

Light tank company

The *Leichte Panzerkompanie* (le PzKp – light tank company) was to have a *Sonder* (Sd – special) structure; KStN 1171(Sd). The HQ section was

Below:
Vehicles of PzGrenDiv Großdeutschland on a dirt track: A PzKpfw III Ausf J from the regimental staff section passes a SdKfz 251/6 from the armoured reconnaissance battalion. The armoured half-track is fitted with a *Sterantenne* (star antenna) 'd' for long-range radio communications.

supplied with a PzKpfw II and a PzKpfw III; the platoon was equipped with five PzKpfw II. There were also three platoons, each with five PzKpfw III.

Medium tank company

The *Mittlere Panzerkompanie* (m PzKp – medium tank company) was also formed to a special structure; KStN 1175 (Sd). The HQ section was supplied with with two PzKpfw IV, and supported by a platoon equipped with five PzKpfw II. Also there were a further three platoons, each with four PzKpfw IV.

May 1940 – meeting reality

After the French campaign, the number of tank divisions was nearly doubled by using a simple ploy. The brigade level was eliminated (with the exception of 3.PzDiv and 10.PzDiv), leaving only one Panzer regiment in the division. The number of tanks decreased significantly, the obsolete PzKpfw I tanks were withdrawn from front-line service, and smaller numbers of the PzKpfw II remained in service.

Below:
In April/May 1943, orders were issued for *Panzerschürzen* (side skirts) to be fitted to all German tanks and self-propelled assault guns. Kits of parts were issued to front-line units for fitting by workshop units when time allowed or during maintenance.

Left:
A number of PzKpfw III
Ausf L tanks from 13.PzDiv
parked in the open terrain of
southern Russia. The tactical
number '801' indicates
that it is the mount of the
commander of 8.Kp. Also
there are a number of SdKfz
250 from the *Kradschützen*
battalion which provided
reconnaissance and infantry
support for the division.

In early 1941 the inconsistency was revealed: All 1.PzDiv, 9.PzDiv, 11.PzDiv, 13.PzDiv, 14.PzDiv, and 16.PzDiv had two medium and four light tank companies. The following; 3.PzDiv, 6.PzDiv, 8.PzDiv, 12.PzDiv, 17.PzDiv, 18.PzDiv, 19.PzDiv, and 20.PzDiv had three medium and six light PzKp. Both 4.PzDiv and 10.PzDiv had two medium and six light tank companies. Finally, 7.PzDiv had three medium and nine light tank companies.

The establishment with PzKpfw III had grown considerably, the majority being armed with the more effective 5cm KwK L/42. But a surprisingly large number of units (6.PzDiv, 7.PzDiv, 8.PzDiv, 12.PzDiv, 19.PzDiv and 20.PzDiv) were still issued with PzKpfw 35(t) and PzKpfw 38(t) armed with the 3.7cm KwK. The number of support tanks (PzKpfw IV) was not increased.

However, this would change in April 1942 when the PzKpfw IV Ausf G mounting the highly effective long-barrelled 7.5cm KwK 40 L/43 entered service, and would become the most important and powerful German tank. Initially deliveries of the PzKpfw IV Ausf G began at a slow rate; an average of only 10 to 12 had been delivered to each Panzer division by July 1942.

Deliveries of the type continued at a slow pace until the end of the year. Prior to the battle for Kursk only one Panzer division (4.PzDiv) had a full complement of PzKpfw IV Ausf G.

In 1943, the PzKpfw V Panther medium tank entered front-line service. This modern vehicle was intended to be far superior to all the types in service with Allied forces. Initially the type was only issued to *Heerestruppen* (army group) units.

However, after German forces were defeated at Kursk a new organizational structure, the PzDiv 43 was introduced. The new Panzer division was to have two battalions, each with four *mittlerer Panzer-Kompanie* (m PzKp – medium tank companies). Ideally, I.Abt would be issued with 88 PzKpfw V Panther tanks, and II.Abt with 88 PzKpfw IV. The ultimate aim was for every Panzer division to be equipped with the Panther. However this was never achieved.

Note: In late 1942, a limited number of PzKpfw VI Ausf E Tiger heavy tanks entered service. Intended as a breakthrough weapon used at focal points of an attack, the type was issued only to *schwere Panzer-Abteilungen* (s PzAbt – heavy tank battalions) deployed at army group level, and not as an integral part of a Panzer division. However, as always, there were exceptions: PzGrenDiv Großdeutschland (GD) and three SS divisions, 1.SS-PzDiv Leibstandarte-SS Adolf Hitler (LSSAH), 2.SS-PzDiv Das Reich (DR) and 3.SS-PzDiv Totenkopf were equipped with the PzKpfw VI Tiger Ausf E.

Far right:
The SdKfz 265 *kleine Panzerbefelhswagen* (kl PzBefWg – light armoured command vehicle) originally entered service as a commander's tank. When sufficient medium tanks became available, the light command tanks were withdrawn from front-line duties and issued to the signals battalion.

ARMOURED RIFLE ELEMENT

The *Schützenbrigaden* (motorized rifle brigades) attached to the Panzer divisions were again not uniform.

In May 1940, the situation with individual tank divisions was complex. Not every Panzer division was provided with what was planned in the KStN: one motorized rifle brigade formed of two motorized rifle regiments.

As an example, 1.PzDiv, 2.PzDiv, 3.PzDiv, 6.PzDiv and 8.PzDiv had a motorized rifle brigade formed as a motorized rifle regiment with three motorized rifle battalions and motorcycle-mounted battalion. Whereas 4.PzDiv, 5.PzDiv, 7.PzDiv, 9.PzDiv and 10.PzDiv had a motorized rifle brigade with two motorized rifle regiments, each with two motorized rifle battalions.

Armoured personnel carrier

It was originally planned to equip all companies in rifle battalions with the *Schützenpanzerwagen* (SPw – armoured personnel carriers). The *mittlerer gepanzerter Mannschaftstransportwagen* (m gep MTW – medium armoured personnel carrier) was built on the chassis of the *mittlerer Zugkraftwagen* (m ZgKw – medium half-track tractor), SdKfz 11. The superstructure of the vehicle was fabricated from sloped armour plates: 14.5mm (front) and 8mm at the sides which gave the occupants protection from infantry fire. Long before the war, a number of variants were in production and included troop carriers, radio and engineer vehicles. The type was designated SdKfz 251.

German industry began to suffer from a shortage of steel and armour plate in the first months of the war. For this reason production of the armoured carrier was divided and an *ungepanzerte* (un-armoured) version was produced.

The *leichter gepanzerter Mannschaftstransportwagen* (le gep MTW – light armoured personnel carrier) was developed in parallel with the medium version. The vehicles were basically similar in appearance, but the le gep MTW was shorter, being built on the chassis of a le ZgKw, SdKfz 10. The vehicle was designated SdKfz 250 and a number of variants were built.

The SdKfz 251 entered service (initially in small numbers) during 1940. Production of the SdKfz 250 commenced in June 1941. Where either type was indicated in early KStNs substitute equipment had to be used.

In May 1940, SchtzRgt 1 in 1.PzDiv was the only unit to receive armoured carriers to equip all of its rifle companies.

SchtzBrig 1 of 1.PzDiv had three rifle battalions in its SchtzBtl 1. Both were supported by a KradSchtzBtl.

Far left:
To provide the *Schützen* (later the Panzer grenadier) companies with fire support, a number of 3.7cm PaK were mounted on the chassis of the SdKfz 251 armoured half-track vehicle. Initially all conversions were carried out by workshop units before the type entered mass production; it was then designated as the SdKfz 215/10.

SchtzRgt 1 as of May 1940

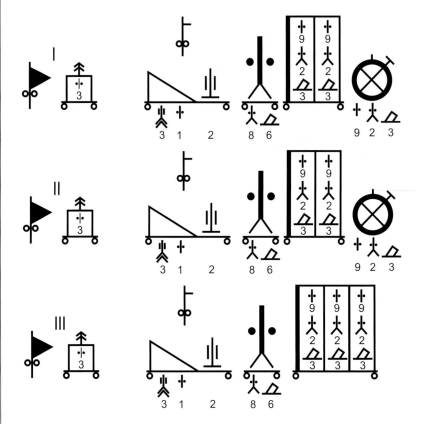

Regimental level

Battalion level

Company level

Support unit level

le InfKol

Rifle regiment

The *Stab eines Schützenregiments* (gep) (rifle regimental staff [armoured]) to KStN 1104, dated 1 October 1937, was a small detachment having five motorcycles and two combinations. The staff section was issued with Kfz 12. In 1940 the staff company was withdrawn.

Signals detachment

The *Nachrichtenzug eines Schützenregiment* (gp) (staff signals detachment [armoured]) was equipped with two motorcycles and a Kfz 15 cross-country vehicle. A number of *Funktruppen* (radio sections) supported the regimental commander:

The *kleiner FunkTruppe* (mot) (kl FuTrp – light radio troop [motorized]) 'c' was equipped with an Kfz 17/1 fitted with a 20W S 'd' transmitter, a Ukw receiver 'F' and a further Ukw receiver 'd1'.

TornFuTrp 'c' (mot) was a detachment equipped with four Kfz 2 fitted with TornFuGer 'c' portable equipment.

kl PzFuTrp 'd' formed as two light radio sections equipped with the SdKfz 261 armoured radio vehicle, fitted with 30W S 'a' transmitter and a TornE 'b' (portable receiver).

Above:
A significant number of SdKfz 10 half-track vehicles were mounted with the 2cm FlaK gun to create a simple but effective self-propelled anti-aircraft weapon: the 2cm FlaK 30 was designated SdKfz 10/4 and the 2cm FlaK 38 as an SdKfz 10/5. Both weapons proved to be very effective against both ground and air targets.

Above:
Vehicles from an artillery
regiment loaded on a
railway wagon. A Kfz 23
Fernsprechkraftwagen
(telephone car) - note the
cable reel mounted on the
mudguard - is on the lead
wagon and a Kfz 17 radio car
is on the second.

Rifle brigade staff

The *Stab eines Schutzenbataillons* (*gepanzerter*) (staff of the rifle battalion
[armoured]) was organized according KStN 1108 (gp) published on
1 October 1939. The HQ section was supplied with two Kfz 15 cross-
country vehicles and provided with six motorcycles for dispatch riders.

Signals detachment

The signals detachment was formed as one kl FernsprTrp (light cable
telephone section) and two TornFuTrp 'd' (portable radio section). The
unit also had two kl PzFuTrp 'a'. It was indicated in all KStN that all the
above were to be issued with the SdKfz 250, but the type had not entered
production when the table was written. The alternative vehicle should have
been the SdKfz 261, but soft-skinned vehicles such as the Kfz 2, Kfz15 or
the Kfz 17 were chosen. This can be confirmed in the files of 6.PzDiv.

Pioneer detachment

A *Panzerpionier Zug* (gep) (PzPioZg – engineer platoon [armoured]) to
KStN 1124 (gp) completed the staff section. One SdKfz 250 (unspecified
variant) was also issued. The platoon had three sections, each equipped with

three SdKfz 251 and a 3-ton truck to carry heavy equipment. The HQ section was issued with three motorcycles, two combinations, and two Kfz 11, Kfz 12 or Kfz 15 cross-country cars.

Motorcycle-mounted rifle company

Two of the three battalions had a *Kradschützen-Kompanie* (KradSchtzKp – motorcycle-mounted rifle company organized according KStN 1111. Each of its three motorcycle platoons had two motorcycles, two Kfz 15 and five combinations. The combinations were fitted with a *Maschinengewehr* (MG – machine gun) 34 and carried a 5cm *Grenatwerfer* (Gw – mortar). There was a further heavy machine gun section equipped with ten combinations each mounting an MG 34. The HQ section was issued with three motorcycles, one combination and also two cross-country cars.

The company trains were assembled from six light trucks, a Kfz 15 cross-country car and a number of motorcycles.

Armoured rifle company

The *Schützenkompanie* (gep) (SchtzKp – rifle company [armoured]) to KStN 1114 (gp) was the mainstay of the battalion. The HQ section was

Above:
One of the most important medium trucks in German service was the Mercedes-Benz L 3000 which entered production in 1938. Although not designed as a cross-country vehicle, its performance was considered more than adequate. A total of some 27,700 had been produced by 1945.

issued with three motorcycles, two motorcycle combinations, and it was planned for the section to have a SdKfz 250/3 (see above). Each company had three rifle platoons equipped with a motorcycle and four SdKfz 251/1 armoured personnel carriers. Other than infantry weapons, the vehicles carried an MG 34, two heavy MG 42 and three 5cm mortars.

The company train was comparable to that of the KradSchtzKp.

Machine-gun company (gp)

The *Maschinengewehr-Kompanie* (gp) (machine gun company [armoured]) to KStN 1116 (gp) had a similar HQ section to the above, but with two SdKfz 250/2 *Fernsprechwagen* (FernsprWg – telephone line-layer vehicle).

The two machine-gun platoons were each issued with two SdKfz 250 and two SdKfz 251 carriers mounting an MG 34.

The mortar platoon had an SdKfz 250 and also six SdKfz 251 mounting the 8cm *Granatwerfer* (Gw – mortar).

It is most probable that other vehicles were used due to a lack of half-track carriers.

The company train was comparable to that of the KradSchtzKp.

Heavy armoured company

The *schwere Kompanie* (gep) (s Kp – heavy company [armoured]) to KStN 1121, 1122, 1123 (gp) provided artillery support. Attached to the unit was a *le Fernsprech* (light cable telephone) section equipped with an SdKfz 250/2.

Right:
Riflemen gather next to an SdKfz 250/3 light armoured radio car. The radio operator wears a *Luftwaffe*-style helmet which indicates that the vehicle is equipped with an Fu 7 radio for air-to-ground communications.

Left:
The Kfz 69 was the standard towing vehicle for light anti-tank or anti-aircraft guns. As a troop carrier it could carry up to eight men and their equipment. But the vehicle was mechanically complex and easily damaged.

The *Panzerabwehr-Zug* (anti-tank platoon) was equipped with three 3.7cm PaK towed by the SdKfz 251/10 and also a SdKfz 250/6 to carry ammunition. The platoon was also supplied with two motorcycles.

The *Infanteriegeschütz-Zug* (infantry gun platoon) was issued with two 7.5cm *leichte Infanteriegeschütz* (le IG) 18 light infantry guns which were towed by SdKfz 251.

The *Leichte Infanterie Kolonne* (light transport column) was supplied with three combinations, two cars and 16 light trucks. This provision could vary, being dependent on availability. The HQ section had three motorcycles, two combinations and a SdKfz 250/3 *Funkwagen*.

Motorcycle rifle battalions

Other than three rifle battalions, the rifle regiment had a further highly mobile element, the *Kradschützen-Bataillon* (KradSchtzBtl – motorcycle-mounted rifle battalion) formed as follows: A staff section, two motorcycle rifle companies, a motorcycle machine-gun company and also a heavy

Right:
Panzer grenadier units were issued with specialized armoured half-track vehicles. These included the SdKfz 251/21, a self-propelled anti-aircraft vehicle which was armed with either 1.5cm or 2cm light cannons in a *drilling* (triple) mounting.

Above:
The SdKfz 251/8, *mittlerer Krankenpanzerwagen* (m KrPzWg – medium armoured ambulance) was fitted to carry four stretcher-borne casualties or a larger number of seated wounded.

Left:
The superstructure of an SdKfz 231, heavy armoured car, was not designed to withstand a direct hit from a heavy weapon. This vehicle was probably hit by an artillery shell which has shattered a section of the armoured body.

Left:
Mobility was the key element
of the Panzer division,
in particular for the rifle
battalions. In the period
before armoured half-track
personnel carriers became
available, trucks were the
only means of transport.
An important type was the
2.5-ton Henschel *Typ* 33 D1,
six-wheeled (four driven)
cargo vehicle, but it lacked
cross-country performance.

company. The staff section was equipped with five motorcycles, three combinations and two Kfz 15.

Signals detachment

The signals detachment to KStN 1109 was equipped with a Kfz 15. The two kl FernsprTrp (light cable telephone section) used a specially adapted Kfz 15/1. A Kfz 2 was issued as transport for the two TornFuTrp 'd' (portable radio section). A SdKfz 261 was issued to the kl PzFuTrp (30W S 'a' transmitter and Torn E 'b') to provide long-range communications. If an armoured vehicle was unavailable, then the unit was authorized to use a soft-skinned vehicle such as the Kfz 17.

The HQ section had a small maintenance section equipped with a Kfz 15, a motorcycle and four light trucks. The train section used three motorcycles, two light cars and four light trucks. A Kfz 31 ambulance followed the column.

Below:
A column of Panzer grenadiers issued with SdKfz 251/1 *Schützenpanzerwagen* (armoured infantry carrier) supported by an SdKfz 251/9 *Kanonenwagen*. An SdKfz 251/21 is positioned to provide fire protection on the flank.

Motorcycle company

The staff section of a *Kradschützen-Kompanie* (motorcycle-mounted company) was issued with three motorcycles, one combination and two Kfz 15 cross-country vehicles.

The motorcycle platoons were the main force. Each had a HQ section which was issued with two motorcycles, a Kfz 11 light cross-country car and a Kfz 15 medium cross-country car. Three combat platoons were issued with 11 combinations, each mounting two MG 34 and carrying a 5cm GrWrf mortar. A fourth platoon, the machine gun platoon, had ten combinations and each mounted two MG 34 machine guns.

The company train consisted of two motorcycles, Kfz 15 and six light trucks.

Heavy company

The *schwere Kompanie* (mot) (s Kp – heavy company [motorized]) to KStN 1121 provided artillery support. The HQ section was issued with

Above:
Motorcycle combinations were light enough to be manhandled out of a difficult situation. Although space was limited, the combination carried equipment and mounted an MG 34. This weapon could be taken off and fitted on a heavy mounting (visible inside the sidecar) and fired from a ground position.

two motorcycles, two combinations and also a Kfz 15. The company train followed the same pattern as other units.

The *Panzerabwehr-Zug* (anti-tank platoon) to KStN 1122: The HQ section was supplied with a Kfz 69 and also two motorcycles for dispatch riders. The anti-tank gun section was equipped with three 3.7cm PaK towed by Kfz 69 light gun tractors. Ammunition for the guns was also carried in a Kfz 69.

The HQ section of the *Infanteriegeschütz-Zug* (infantry gun platoon) to KStN 1123 was issued with a motorcycle and two combinations and also a Kfz 15. The unit's two 7.5cm *leichter Infanteriegeschütz* (leIG – light infantry gun) 18 were towed by a Kfz 69, with ammunition carried also in a Kfz 69.

The HQ section of the *Pionier-Zug* (engineer platoon) to KStN 1124 was provided with two motorcycles, two combinations, three Kfz 15 and also two 3-ton trucks.

Below:
An SdKfz 250/1 appears overloaded with a *Kradschützen* unit as it negotiates a railway embankment: the *Schützenpanzerwagen* was considered to be the safest means of transporting infantry around all battle grounds.

Left:
German troops have positioned two pieces of channel-sectioned steel to allow a *Kradschützen* unit to cross a destroyed bridge. To reduce weight the MG 34 has been dismounted.

Right:
A rifle company of 1.PzDiv equipped with SdKfz 251 during the initial phase of the invasion of Russia. All the half-tracks are carrying fascines (bundles of thick tree branches) which were laid over marsh-like terrain – common in Russia – to prevent the non-driven front wheels sinking into the mud. (SZ Photo)

Right:
A number of SdKfz 250/1 in service with the *Kradschützen-Kompanie* of SS-Div Großdeutschland. It appears that all are fitted with FuSprech 'f' radio equipment. Interestingly, the lead vehicle is fitted with a non-standard body of the type used for the SdKfz 253: note the hole for the pivot-type aerial has been welded over.

Left:
A concentration of light armoured personnel carriers hidden from enemy observation in a low depression. Two are standard SdKfz 251/1 and two are mounting the MG 34, but without a gun shield. Also there is an SdKfz 250/10 mounting a 3.7cm PaK anti-tank gun.

Left:
Engineers have erected a bridge over a deep stream, but it did not have sufficient capacity to carry a medium tank. As a result, the commander of this PzKpfw IV Ausf E of PzRgt 25 in 7.PzDiv has attempted to make a crossing only to become bogged down. A recovery team has attached steel-wire cables to another PzKpfw IV to haul the tank back onto firm ground. An SdKfz 253 from the divisional artillery regiment crosses the bridge safely.

ARTILLERY-REGIMENT (MOT)

The *Artillerie-Regiment* (artillery element) was one of the largest subunits, in both equipment and personnel, of a Panzer division. The artillery regiment was formed as two light battalions and a heavy battalion.

German military planners in the 1930s considered artillery to be of utmost importance to the army, but other nations thought differently. France, Russia and Great Britain respectively introduced smaller calibre field guns – Canon de 75 mle 1897, 76mm divisional gun M 1936 and the Ordnance QF 25pdr – which, although not powerful, were extremely versatile. German military planners, after a careful evaluation of the above types, decided to order 24 of the 10.5cm *leichter Feldhaubitz* (le FH) 18, a light field howitzer.

If the artillery was to keep pace with a highly mobile Panzer division or the mechanized infantry divisions it would have to be motorized. German planners were aware of the many advantages of a rapid artillery force and began to work on the problem. The simplest way to motorize the artillery would be to utilize and adapt the powerful half-tracked prime movers that were currently in service. It was also realized that forward artillery observers would require light armoured vehicles. But due to the critical supply situation nothing had been produced by the end of 1940.

A 15cm *schwere Feldhaubitz* (sFH – heavy field howitzer) 18 was produced for service with heavy artillery battalions.

However a few heavy, low-trajectory (flat-fire) guns were available in the Panzer division. The s 10cm *Kanone* (K – cannon) 18, (true calibre was 10.5cm), was in service and each heavy battalion was supplied with four. In October 1941 the majority of tank divisions, including 1.PzDiv, would lose their K 18 battery, having it replaced by a third battery equipped with the 15cm s FH 18. But a short time later, the K 18 was returned as it was found that low-trajectory fire was indispensable.

Staff

The *stab eines artillerie-regiments* (staff of the artillery regiment) had an HQ section organized according to KStN 411. It was issued with four motorcycles, a light car, four Kfz 15 and a medium passenger coach which was used as a command post.

The regimental *Nachrichtenzug* (signals platoon), to KStN 561, was attached to the divisional signals battalion. The HQ section was issued with a combination and a Kfz 17/1 radio vehicle, equipped as a kl FuTrp 'c' (20W S 'a', Ukw E 'd', Torn E 'b' portable receiver).

For cable telephone communications, three kl FernSprTrp (light

Far left:
The SdKfz 250/5, *leichter Panzerbeobachtungswagen* (le BeobPzWg – armoured observation vehicle) was issued to armoured artillery regiments. The type was fitted with a 30W Fu 8 radio to provided communications with divisional staff sections. The vehicle was armed with two MG 42 machine guns.

Far right:
The artillery regiment of a Panzer division in 1940 was reliant on three types of gun to equip each of its batteries. Two were each issued with four 15cm sFH 18, one battery was issued with four s 10cm K 18 and six batteries each issued with four 10.5cm le FH 18.

telephone section) were supplied with Kfz 15; the gr FernSprTrp 'a' (heavy telephone section) had a Kfz 2 and also a Horch-built Kfz 23 FernSprKw (telephone car). Also available were two Kfz 17 fitted as a kl FuTrp 'b' (mot) on). The radio provision was completed by one kl FuTrp 'c' (mot) carried in a Kfz 17/1. The four TornFuTrp 'b' (portable radio section) were transported in Kfz 2.

A *Wettertrupp* (meteorological section), to KStN 531, provided weather forecasts for the ground forces. The section was equipped with a motorcycle and a Kfz 62 *Wetterkraftwagen* (weather van), which carried meteorological equipment, built on the chassis of a le gl Lkw (o). [Note: Kfz 62 was assigned for at least seven different purposes).

The *Felddruckereizug* (printing section), to KStN 527, was issued with a motorcycle, a light cross-country car, a medium truck and a Kfz 62 *Druckereikraftwagen* (printer's truck), [see above].

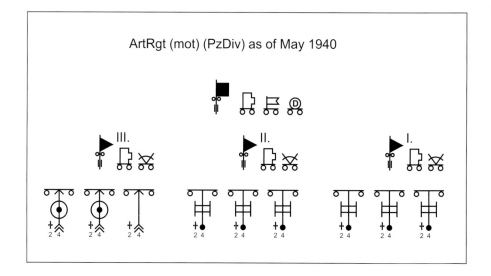

ArtRgt (mot) (PzDiv) as of May 1940

Far right:
The s 10cm K 18 was a low-trajectory gun intended to complement the heavy 15cm howitzer. The gun provided the artillery regiment with a long-range ability since it could fire on a target some 19,000m distant. Only the length of the barrel distinguished it from the sFH 18.

Light artillery battalion staff

The *stab einer leichten artillerieabteilung* (staff of a light artillery battalion) consisted of the HQ section, to KStN 413, resp 406, the battalion workshop section and a small number of trucks.

The HQ section was issued with three motorcycles, two combinations, one light cross-country car and two Kfz 12.

The *Instandsetzungstaffel* (workshop section) had one combination, one le Pkw and three light trucks. The train section was issued with a combination and four further light trucks.

The *Nachrichtenzug* (signals platoon) *for an Artillerieabteilung* (artillery battalion) was responsible for telephone and radio communication. The HQ section was provided with three motorcycles, and a combination and two Kfz 12.

Three sections were responsible for telephone communication: m FernSprTrp 'b' was issued with a Kfz 15 and also a Kfz 77 *Fernsprechkraftwagen* (FernSprKfz – radio-equipped van). The gr FernSprTrp 'c' had a Kfz 2 and also a Kfz 77 FernSprKfz. The kl FernSprTrp 'c' was supplied with Kfz 15.

For cable telephone communications, three kl FernSprTrp were issued with the Kfz 15: A gr FernSprTrp 'a' (heavy telephone section) used a Kfz 2 and also a Kfz 23 FernSprKw (telephone car). The exact types of vehicle issued very much depended on availability.

The staff section was supported by six TornFuTrp 'b' (portable radio section); of these three were issued with the Kfz 2, and the other three would be transported on any available vehicles.

Below:
A radio operator operating a TornFu 'd2' transceiver: This portable radio had a voice range of 10km and was used by all services, including the artillery.

An *Artillerie-Vermessungstrupp* (artillery surveyor section) was provided with two motorcycles and a Kfz 3. This was a specialized vehicle built on the chassis of a commercial light car or light truck to carry surveying equipment.

Light field howitzer battery

The *batterie leichter feldhaubitzen* (light field howitzer battery) was equipped with four guns, in accordance to KStN 434. The battery was formed as a HQ section, a gun section, two ammunition sections and supply/cargo train.

The *Batterietrupp* (battery troop) was supplied with a Kfz 11 half-track vehicle and three motorcycles. There was also a Kfz 12 manned by specially trained NCOs equipped with the *Scherenfernrohr* (scissor-type periscope). The forward observer was supplied with a motorcycle combination. According an army bulletin (article 754, issue 1940), each battery was authorized to have two, either an SdKfz 253 or an SdKfz 254 armoured observer vehicle. It is most probable that forward observers used other vehicles including the combination.

Above:
As a result of the *Anschluss* (annexation) of Austria in 1938, the *Wehrmacht* commandeered a significant amount of military equipment. The Saurer RK 7, a wheel-cum-track design, was standardized as the SdKfz 254 *mittlerer gepanzerter Beobachtungswagen* (m gep BeobWg – medium armoured observation vehicle). In German service the vehicle was fitted with Fu 6 and Fu 2 radios.

The *Nachrichtenstaffel* (signals detachment) had a gr FernSprTrp 'a' issued with a Kfz 2/2 and also a Kfz 77 *Fernsprechkraftwagen*. The detachment's m FernSprTrp 'b' was equipped with a Kfz 15 and a Kfz 77. Three different sections provided cable telephone communications: gr FernSprTrp 'c' relied on a Kfz 2 and also a Kfz 77. The kl FernSprTrp 'c' was provided with a Kfz 15. A Kfz 2 was used to carry TornFuTrp 'f' (portable transceiver); two other transceivers were carried on other vehicles in the battery.

The HQ section of the *Geschützstaffel* (gun detachment) was supplied with two motorcycles, three Kfz 12 and a Kfz 4, anti-aircraft vehicle. The four 10.5cm le Fh 18 were towed by an SdKfz 6 half-track tractor.

Two *Munitionsstaffel* (ammunition detachments) were issued with three motorcycles, a combination, a light cross-country car, eight 3-ton trucks and four ammunition trailers.

The *Tross* (train) was supplied with two motorcycles, two light trucks and two 3-ton trucks. An SdKfz 6 was kept in reserve as a spare vehicle.

Heavy field howitzer battery

Beside the two light field howitzer battalions, the regiment had a third (heavy) battalion issued with 15cm s FH 18 and/or the s 10cm K 18.

To tow the heavy guns the third battalion was issued with the SdKfz 7 half-track tractor.

Far left:
The 7.5cm *leichter Infanterie-Geschütz* (leIG – light infantry gun) 18 was standard equipment for the rifle companies and associated units. The type had a range of up to 3,500m and fired high-explosive (HE) ammunition. It could also fire hollow-charge rounds to combat enemy tanks.

Left:
A gun crew from ArtRgt 88 in 18.PzDiv prepares a 10.5cm *leichter Feldhaubitz* (leFH – light field howitzer) 18. The gun, which had a maximum range of 10,600m, was the standard artillery weapon. For transport it would be towed by either an SdKfz 11 or an SdKfz 6 half-track tractor.

ANTI-TANK BATTALION

The *Panzerjäger-Abteilung* (PzAbt – anti-tank battalion) was an important integral element of a Panzer division. The name *Panzerjäger* clearly indentifies its original task; not the defence against enemy tanks, but to actively seek and destroy. But the *Panzerjäger* were often compelled to fight enemy anti-tank troops hindering an attack by a German tank brigade.

On many occasions the *Panzerjäger* were called on to support an infantry assault by attacking the enemy positions with high-explosive (HE) fire. Heavy *Panzerjäger* units (in 1940 most units had the 3.7cm PaK), were beginning to be equipped with small numbers of self-propelled 8.8cm guns.

The staff section of the battalion included support elements and three combat companies each armed with 12 of the 3.7cm PaK.

Staff section

The *Gruppe Führer* (HQ section), to KStN 110, was issued with a motorcycle and three combinations. The battalion commander was issued with a Kfz 21;

Far left:
In 1940 the 3.7cm PaK was the standard anti-tank gun in German service. Normally it was towed by a medium cross-country car or a light truck, but when used by a rifle regiment it would be hitched to an SdKfz 251. The vehicle shown is the *ungepanzerter* (un-armoured) version in service with 1.PzDiv.

Below:
The 8.8cm *Flugzeugabwehrkanone* (FlaK – anti-aircraft gun): The army trained the crews in its FlaK units to use the weapon against ground targets.

Above:
A pre-war *Kübelsitzwagen* (bucket-seat vehicle); the simple bodywork was mounted on a modified chassis of a civilian passenger car. By 1939 the vehicle, sometimes referred to as Kfz 1, had almost been phased out of military service.

Right:
When it entered service, the performance of the 3.7cm PaK anti-tank gun was comparable to other European weapons. It was designed to be light enough to be hauled by its crew. The gun shield gave protection against armour-piercing infantry ammunition.

his deputy and the battalion *Amtsarzt* (medical officer) were provided with either a Kfz 12 or 15 cross-country vehicle.

The *Gefechtstross* (combat train), *Verpflegungstross* (rations train) and the *Gepäcktross* (baggage train) were issued with a similarly composed number and combination of vehicles: a Kfz 12 and four light trucks. A further section was the *Hilfsstaffel* (support detachment), which was part of the workshop elements.

The staff section included an SdKfz 77 *Krankenwagen* (ambulance), the *Feldküche* (field kitchen) and other important elements.

Signals platoon

As noted in the files of 6.PzDiv, the signals platoon for a PzJgAbt was issued with two motorcycles, two Kfz 15 and six Kfz 2/2, with up to another seven of the type for the TornFuTrp 'b' (portable radio section): a clear contradiction to KStN 1192. Interestingly, the structure for 6.PzDiv shows that two kl PzFuTrp 'c' were equipped with the SdKfz 261. But these radio-equipped armoured cars were not available and were replaced by the Kfz 17. A note from the unit commander states that he thought the Kfz 17 soft-skinned van was totally unsuitable.

Anti-tank company

The standard *Panzerjäger-Kompanie* (mot) (PzJgKp – anti-tank company [motorized]), to KStN 1141, was formed as a HQ section, three anti-tank platoons and the usual train.

The commander of the *Kompanietrupp* (HQ) was issued with a Kfz 12: the company was supplied with four motorcycles. The three *Panzerjäger-Zug* (PzJgZg – anti-tank platoon) were each provided with a Kfz 12 and two motorcycles. The anti-tank guns were towed by Kfz 69 gun tractors and another two Kfz 69 were used to tow ammunition trailers and also served as reserve vehicles.

The *Tross* (train/convoy) consisted of a Kfz 12, two combinations, four light trucks and a medium truck.

But the files of 6.PzDiv again show a number of anomalies: The division was issued with a larger number of Kfz 12 or Kfz 15 vehicles and also an increased number of trucks. However the Kfz 69 towing vehicles were replaced by the more powerful SdKfz 10, half-track vehicle tractor.

The above shows a change which was applied to all KStN published from early 1941. This structure showed alternative provision with either the Kfz 12 type A (for anti-tank companies in infantry divisions), Kfz 69 type B or the SdKfz 10 type C, for anti-tank companies in tank divisions).

Left:
Two subunits of a Panzer division on parade: In the foreground are the vehicles, SdKfz 263 and SdKfz 223, of the motorized reconnaissance battalion. Behind them are a number of Krupp Protze towing 3.7cm PaK anti-tank guns from the tank destroyer battalion.

Above:

In 1940, German military planners decided that the 7.5cm PaK 40 would be the standard anti-tank gun and as the war progressed it would be mounted on a number of different tank chassis. An SdKfz 138, Marder II is being driven into the cargo hold of a Me 323, the six-engine transport aircraft.

Left:
The 5cm PaK 38 was thought to be the logical successor to the 3.7cm PaK anti-tank gun. Development began shortly before outbreak of war, but the type proved to be ineffective against Russian heavy tanks. Shown is a 5cm PaK 38, in service with the rifle regiment of 15.PzDiv in North Africa, attached to an SdKfz 251.

Left:
In early 1940, German military planners decided to order the production of a self-propelled anti-tank gun capable of defeating French heavy tanks. The PzKpfw I chassis was selected as a base for the vehicle on which to mount a Czech-built 4.7cm PaK anti-tank gun.

SIGNALS BATTALION

The *Nachrichten-Abteilung* (signals battalion) was another vital element in a Panzer division. Due to this unit being high mobile it was issued with more radio but less cable telephone equipment. Unlike a signals unit in an infantry division, the *Panzer-Nachrichten-Abteilung* (PzNachrAbt – armoured radio battalion) was issued with an increased number of armoured vehicles to enable it to keep pace with an attack by armoured elements.

Staff section

The staff section, to KStN 807, consisted of the *Gruppe Führer* (HQ section) issued with three motorcycles, a Kfz 12, three Kfz 15, a light truck and three 3-ton trucks. A *Hilfsstaffel* (support detachment) was attached to the workshop element and was issued with a motorcycle, a Kfz 15 and four trucks.

Armoured signals company

One of the main bodies of the signals battalion was the *Panzer-Nachichten-Kompanie* (PzNachrKp – armoured signals company), to KStN 981. It provided strong cable telephone material and radio equipment.

The *Kompaniestab* (company HQ) was issued with two motorcycles, one combination, one Kfz 15 and one light truck. A *Hilfstrupp* (support squad) provided technical services; it was issued with two Kfz 15 and a combination.

1. Platoon: This had a HQ section equipped with a Kfz 15 and two motorcycles, the m PzFuTrp 'b' was issued with a Kfz 15 and also an SdKfz 263. The NachrTrp 'a' (telephone section) had a Kfz 15 and a Kfz 17.

Far left:
The TonFu 'g' was a portable transceiver which, when fitted with a 1.5m whip-type aerial, had a voice range of between 6km and 12km, but this was dependent on where it was positioned and weather conditions.

Left:
The SdKfz 267 and 268 *Panzerbefehlswagen* III command vehicles were used throughout the war. The type was fitted with a wooden replica of a 5cm gun and a *Maschinengewehr* (MG – machine gun) 34 for self defence.

Left:
This radio team has been
issued with a French-built
Renault Chenilette UE
light tractor to carry their
equipment. The radio is
a Torn Fu 'b1' portable
transceiver which had a
voice range of up to 12km.

Right:
The Büssing-NAG G 31, classified as light cross-country vehicle, was built in a number of variants until 1935. One of the most common was the Kfz 61 *Funkkraftwagen*. The vehicle is fitted with a telescopic mast aerial which indicates that it is equipped with long-range radios.

The two NachrTrp 'b' (telephone section) were provided with a Kfz 15. The gr NachrTrp 'a' (heavy telephone section) was issued with a Kfz 2/1 and also a Kfz 77. The platoon also had the use of several motorcycles.

2.Platoon: The unit had a HQ section, which was provided with a Kfz 15 and two motorcycles. The four gr NachrTrp 'a' (heavy telephone section) used a Kfz 2/1 and also a Kfz 77. The unit also had a number of motorcycles.

3.Platoon: This unit had a HQ section, which was equipped with Kfz 15 and two motorcycles. The m PzFuTrp 'b' was issued with a Kfz 15 and also an SdKfz 263. Four SdKfz 261 were allotted to kl PzFuTrp 'd'. The telephone units: NachrTrp 'a' had a Kfz 15 and also a Kfz 17: the heavy gr NachrTrp 'a' was supplied with a Kfz 2/1 and also a Kfz 77. All four NachrTrp 'b' were equipped with the Kfz 15. Again, the platoon also had a number of motorcycles at its disposal.

Combat train

The *Gefechtsstaffel* (combat train) was issued with two motorcycles, a Kfz 2 and a Kfz 42 *Nachrichtenwerkstattwagen* (signals workshop truck). An important piece of equipment was a *schwere Maschinen-Satz* 'A' (s MaschSatz – heavy machinery [generator] set) mounted on a single-axle trailer (SdAnh 24). Six light trucks were used to carry all other equipment.

Radio company

The second company was the *PanzerFunk-Kompanie* (PzFuKp – armoured radio company), to KStN 971, was equipped with long-range and air-to-ground radio equipment.

The *Kompaniestab* (company HQ) was issued with two motorcycles, a combination, a Kfz 15 and also light truck. A *Hilfstrupp* (support section) provided mechanical services and was equipped with two Kfz 15 and a combination.

Left:
The SdKfz 263 *Panzerfunkwagen*, armoured radio car, was issued to the reconnaissance and signal units in Panzer divisions. The vehicle was fitted with either m PzTrp 'a' or 'b' (mot) radio equipment. The SdKfz 263 is fitted with the large frame-type antenna, but a *Kürbelmast* (extendable from 8 to 10m) has been erected to allow communications at maximum range.
(SZ Photo)

Above:
The SdKfz 251/6 *Kommandowagen* (KdoWg - command vehicle) was fitted with different types of radio equipment. When used by a divisional commander it would be fitted with an Fu 19 short-wave radio and an Fu 12 medium-wave radio.

1.Platoon: The HQ section was issued with a Kfz 15 and two motorcycles. The unit had four air-to-ground liaison vehicles, three SdKfz 267 and an SdKfz 268. The kl PzFuTrp 'c' had an SdKfz 260. Also equipped with the same vehicle were the six kl PzFuTrp 'd'.

2.Platoon: As with 1.Platoon, the HQ section was provided with Kfz 15 and two motorcycles. Each of the six m FuTrp 'b' sections was issued with a Kfz 15 and an SdKfz 263.

3.Platoon: Like the other units the HQ section was provided with Kfz 15 and two motorcycles. The unit also had two SdKfz 267 and an SdKfz 268 air-to-ground liaison vehicle. An SdKfz 260 was issued to kl PzFuTrp 'c'.

Combat train

The *Gefechtsstaffel* (combat train) was almost identical to that of the PzNachrKp.

Transport column

The *Transportkolonne* (transport column), to KStN 991, was formed of a combination, a Kfz 12, five light trucks and also a Kfz 42. Also an s MaschSatz A on SdAnh 24 generator set was included.

Note: The range of vehicles available to the PzNachrAbt was almost the same as that provided for all elements in a Panzer division and much depended on availability. There was a shortage of many specialized vehicles, such as the PzBefWg variant of the PzKpfw III, and the SdKfz 260, SdKfz 261 also the SdKfz 263 armoured cars. On many occasions these important vehicles had to be substituted by other soft-skinned radio-equipped vehicles. The SdKfz 265 *kleine Panzerbefehlswagen* (kl PzBefWg – light commander's vehicle) was also frequently used.

Below:
The French-built Renault AH was a standard 4.5-ton truck. Vast numbers were captured after the Fall of the France, and production continued during the German occupation. The vehicle is in service with 5.PzDiv in Russia and has been camouflaged with brushed-on white paint.

Right:
Telephone operators in
front of *Klappenschränke*
(telephone switchboard).
Exchanges like this were
used by higher echelons,
such as army group
command, to keep in contact
with support services in rear
positions.

ANTI-AIRCRAFT COMPANY (MOT)

In World War II aircraft capable of ground attack posed an obvious risk. Although specialized types had not been developed by 1940 (with the exception of the German Ju-87 Stuka), a unit such as the Panzer division still needed an anti-aircraft defence.

Military planners identified the problem and ordered the development of anti-aircraft artillery which would become an integrated element of tank divisions. However, all anti-aircraft artillery came under the command of the *Luftwaffe* and they would operate the units.

The Order of Battle published in 1939 shows that not one of the divisions in service had an anti-aircraft element. But around September 1939, *Flugzeugabwehrkanone-Abteilungen* (FlaK-Abt – anti-aircraft battalions) were being attached to each army corps, and all Panzer divisions, including the light divisions, received a *leichte FlaK-Abteilung* (light anti-aircraft battalion).

An after-action report published in November 1939 noted that this provision was felt to be sufficient. However, after the invasion of France, where the rapid advance left many defensive forces behind, all anti-aircraft units were reduced to company strength. But total protection from air attack over the battlefront would never be achieved.

After annihilation of the Polish air force, German anti-aircraft units were increasingly called on to support other units in ground combat. The *General der Luftwaffe* accepted this, but was never happy with this type of commitment.

Far left:
The 8.8cm *Flugzeugabwehrkanone* (FlaK – anti-aircraft gun) was designed to defeat enemy aircraft flying at medium to high altitude. German forces recognized its true potential and used it as a multi-purpose artillery weapon.

Below:
In 1943, growing Allied air superiority forced Germany to produce the *Flakpanzer* (armoured anti-aircraft vehicle) of which three types were built using a PzKpfw IV chassis: *Möbelwagen* (furniture van) mounted a 3.7cm FlaK 43 L/60 or four 2cm Vierling 38 L/55; *Ostwind* (east wind) mounted 3.7cm FlaK 43 L/60 and *Wirbelwind* (whirlwind) which mounted four 2cm Vierling L/55.

In March 1940, the *Oberkommando der Wehrmacht* (OKW – army high command) reported the number of FlaKAbt in service with the army:

22 FlaKAbt
11 le FlaKAbt

In theory, the number of light anti-aircraft battalions would have been sufficient to equip ten Panzer divisions. However a valid KStN, dated October 1940, authorized FlaK forces in company strength for a Panzer division. A FlaK company, listed in KStN 192, was attached to a *Panzerjäger-Abteilung* and placed under the control of the unit's commanding officer.

A FlaK battalion was formed as follows. The *Kompanie-Trupp* (HQ section) was issued with four motorcycles, a light motor car and a Kfz 15. A *Nachrichtenstaffel* (signals section) was provided with a Kfz 2 to transport five TornFuTrp 'b' (portable radio section).

The FlaK company had three combat platoons. The 1.Platoon and 2.Platoon had identical equipment: two motorcycles and two Kfz15. It also had four SdKfz 10/4 mounting 2cm FlaK guns for anti-aircraft air defence, supported by two SdKfz 10 ammunition carriers.

Below:
The 2cm FlaK 38 mounted on an SdKfz 10/5 was also very effective for providing heavy support fire in both attack and defensive operations. The gun had a rate of fire of 420 to 480rpm and fired high-explosive (HE) or armour-piercing (AP) ammunition.

The 3.Platoon was issued with five motorcycles and Kfz 15. It also had two quadruple-mounted 2cm FlaK-Vierling 38 cannons which were towed by 4.5-ton heavy trucks. Ammunition for the guns was carried in two heavy trucks.

The *Gefechtstross* (combat train) was issued with a motorcycle and a combination, also Kfz 15 and four light trucks. The workshop section was equipped with a Kfz 2/4 and a light truck.

The *Verpflegungstross* and *Gepäcktross* (rations and baggage convoys) were issued with three light trucks.

The final establishment dated April 1941, shows that only one 2cm FlaK platoon was equipped with four SdKfz 10/4. The four 2cm guns of the second platoon were towed by Kfz 81 *leichter FlaK-Kraftwagen*. Ammunition was carried in two light trucks.

The third platoon was issued with two SdKfz 7/1 each fitted with a 2cm FlaK-Vierling 38 in a quadruple-mounting. Ammunition was carried by two half-tracks, which also served as replacement vehicles.

The fourth Flak-Vierling 38 platoon had an identical number of guns, but the half-track vehicles were replaced by 4.5-ton trucks.

Above:
A 8.8cm FlaK 18 being towed by an SdKfz 7 over a pioneer-built bridge in Romania as part of the build-up to *Unternehmen* (Operation) Marita; the invasion of the Balkan states.

Above:
The crew of an un-armoured (except for the gun shield) SdKfz 10/5, was not only vulnerable to enemy fire, but they were also exposed to all weather conditions. Note a FlaK-Visier 38 gun sight has been fitted.

Right:
To mobilize their anti-aircraft weapons, many units loaded the guns on any suitable vehicles. Here a 2cm FlaK 30 on a mounting fabricated from wood has been positioned on a light truck.

Above:
The 2cm FlaK-Vierling 38 L/55 quadruple gun was a formidable weapon. The 2,000rpm rate of fire was limited since the gun was fitted with a 20-round magazine. The type was designated SdKfz 7/1.

Left:
Each SdKfz 10/4 (2cm FlaK 30) was supplied with the standard SdAnh 51 trailer which was originally intended to carry the anti-aircraft gun. Instead a box was fitted to carry ammunition and tools.

In 1942 PzArtRgt 74, an integral element of 2.PzDiv, was authorized to have 24 10.5cm *leichter Feldhaubitz* (leFH – light field howitzer) 18 to equip its first and second battalions. The third battalion was equipped with four 10cm *schwere Kanone* (s K – heavy gun) 18 and eight 15cm *schwere Feldhaubitz* (s FH – heavy field howitzer) 18. But over the year the number of guns was significantly reduced.

The following experience report is a perfect example of artillery warfare in World War II.

On 4 August 1942, a strong enemy force succeeded in breaking the German frontline at position 'Barbara'. Consequently 2.PzDiv, attached to XXXVI.Army, was ordered into combat to stop the enemy.

By mid-1942, the Red Army had become numerically, in equipment and manpower, a superior force to the German invaders. Although tactically inexperienced and lacking experienced leaders the Soviets appeared to have an inexhaustible supply of men and armoured vehicles.

During the period covered by the report, PzArtRgt 74 was positioned some 8 to 10km behind the frontline. But due to extenuating circumstances

Below:
All German Panzer divisions were issued with motorized artillery units comprising a heavy battalion equipped with eight 15cm s FH 18 and four s 10 K 18. Each gun would be towed by an SdKfz 7 half-tracked tractor, which not only had good off-road mobility but also allowed the guns to be rapidly redeployed.

it proved necessary to pull the le FH 18 batteries forward; a frequent occurrence in order to fight large formations of Russian tanks. The same applied to the 10cm s K 18 batteries, such was the desperate situation on the frontline.

Experience report from PzArtRgt 74 for the period 9 to 15 August 1942:

9 August 1942

At 08:00hrs the enemy advances from his assembly area near Ljebedni and launches a massive tank assault against our front-line positions near Jelnja. The wooded area 500m northwest of Jelnja is being held by Hauptman Schreiber and a few riflemen along with the Vorgeschober-Beobachter (VB – forward observer) of 4.Bttr. Schreiber was fatally wounded and replaced by Oberleutnant Gündel. During the morning, the forward observer continues to direct fire until his field telephone line is broken. During the battle, his actions have enabled our forces to destroy 13 enemy tanks with armour-piercing weapons.

The gun of Unteroffizier Fessel, positioned slightly ahead of the frontline, was particularly effective and destroyed six enemy tanks. The anti-tank guns of 9.Bttr

Below:
The gun barrel of a 15cm sFH 18 has suffered a *'Rohrkrepierer'* (barrel burst), a constant risk faced by all gunners. It could possibly be caused by damaged or faulty ammunition, insufficient barrel cleaning or extreme temperatures generated by rapid firing; perhaps even sabotage. The shock wave generated by the explosion and the resulting metal splinters could severely injure the crew.

destroyed a further four tanks. In the afternoon, a second gun opens fire from a forward position and destroys another three tanks [T-34 or Mk 3 Valentine]; all were immobilized by the wet ground.

From 09:30 to 12:00hrs Kriwzy, Ryabinki and Shtanino are subjected to a number of heavy attacks by enemy infantry supported by tanks. In response, I.Abt lays down a barrage of defensive fire, but expends almost all of its ammunition. At 20:30hrs, the enemy succeeds in forcing our troops to withdraw and establish a new frontline at the boundary of Ryabinki. Here I.Abt and 7.Bttr succeed in halting the advance. During the battle, the BeobBttr (observation battery) locates the position of four enemy batteries; one is immediately attacked by 8.Bttr.

10 August 1942

Just before dawn, the enemy attack and succeeds in breaking through our front-line positions near Gladkoie. At around 06:00hrs, our tanks launch an attack and regain the positions. The enemy launched another attack, but this is halted by a heavy barrage by the guns of II.Abt and III.Abt which allows our troops to counterattack. The enemy launched several attacks during the day, mainly against our positions at Ryabinki and Gladkoie.

Between 11:35 and 15:00hrs, the enemy launches further assaults on Krivzy supported by tanks, but the attack is halted by a barrage from the guns of I.Abt. At 15:05hrs, the guns of I. and III.Abt repulse an enemy force near Ryabinki.

Although the batteries continue to provide defensive barrages in support of our front-line positions, they also open long-range barrages at enemy assembly areas around Knevo, Podberjeski, Skorozovo and Ramenka.

Below:
The wide open landscape of southern Russia: A battery of four 15cm s FH 18 target Red Army forces positioned several kilometres distant. Note the gun's crew has stored the ammunition some distance from their weapon.

Left:
A 15cm *schwere Feldhaubitz* (s FH – heavy field howitzer) 18 was the mainstay of all German artillery units. Note the gunner's hand wheels and gunsight mounting to the left of the breech block and also the black table detailing ballistic data. Although reliable, the type was outgunned by similar British and Russian weapons.

The sector covered by the guns of II.Abt remains quiet after they devastated enemy forces during the assaults of the previous day. An abandoned T-34 is destroyed 6.Bttr, and a damaged tank is destroyed by a gun of I.Abt.

11 August 1942
The towns of Ryabinki, Gladkoie and Jelnja are again the scene of further violent fighting as several villages repeatedly change hands. The enemy has once again managed to replenish his tank forces.

At 07:15hrs, the guns of I.Abt are ordered to open fire against an attack on Gladkoie; further attacks at 11:15 and 14:40hrs are repelled. A group of 12 enemy tanks are spotted near houses close to Jelnja; the guns of II.Abt and III.Abt open fire, forcing them to retreat. But between 12:00hrs and 15:00hrs, the tanks return and launch further surprise attacks on Jelnja, finally managing to enter the village forcing German troops to retreat from the northern area. The leading gun of 9.Bttr, commanded by *Oberleutnant* Schlanitz, opens fire and destroys two enemy tanks. The enemy infantry following the tanks are engaged by the gun crew and the forward observer, but a counterattack by our infantry causes the enemy to retreat.

During the battle, another three another enemy tanks are destroyed by a gun of 6.Bttr positioned on the northern boundary of Jelnja. A light field howitzer is destroyed by a direct hit and totally destroyed; *Oberleutnant* Melnitzky, the commander, is wounded. Sadly, during the battle Oberleutnant Keil, the deputy adjutant of II.Abt, is fatally wounded.

At around 16:00hrs, the enemy launches another tank assault, but this time concealed by a shallow depression in the terrain to attack Jelnja from a north eastern direction. This time attack is supported by an even larger number of infantry, but our two forward guns are unable to open fire, causing our troops to evacuate Jelnja.

A group led by *Oberstleutnant* Kischke manages to establish a defensive line to the north of the village which allows our artillery to cover a wide front. The guns of 4.Bttr, 5.Bttr and 9.Bttr are not only providing cover for our retreating troops, but are also bombarding the enemy to prevent a further advance.

After arrival of our tanks we launch a counterattack to regain the village and also to retrieve both forward guns. No riflemen were available for this operation; instead our gun crews were carried on the tanks. We managed to recover the gun of 9.Bttr [s 10cm K 18] undamaged but the other, a 10.5cm le FH 18, could not be retrieved since a bridge had been demolished, and the stream was too deep for our tanks to cross.

The enemy attacked our right flank with increased ferocity, menacing Shtanino Ryabinki and Krivzy. A barrage by the guns of I.Abt and 7.Bttr and 8.Bttr successfully halted the attack. The guns of 7.Bttr destroyed a 7.62cm gun, a mortar and a heavy machine-gun position with direct hits.

12 August 1942

The enemy appears to be unable to hold his new front line, as our troops attack, supported by artillery, to reclaim their previous positions.

At around 10:30hrs, the enemy launched a heavy assault against our new frontline deploying ten tanks with mounted infantry. But this fails due to intense fire from the regiment; two enemy tanks are destroyed. The attack, by now dismounted enemy infantry, is halted, leaving many wounded on the battlefield. During the afternoon further enemy tanks and infantry in company strength attack, but are all defeated.

At 16:00hrs, the guns of I.Abt halt an attack by several Russian companies on battalion 'Buck', while the guns of 9.Bttr engage enemy assembly positions near Botolchi. Between 15:25hrs and 17:00hrs, all the guns of the artillery regiment fire several barrages on

concentrations of enemy troops at Kowaliki and also on vehicle parks west of Ovsjaniki. An enemy attack launched at 20:10hrs from Pushkino fails in the face of a barrage by the guns of III.Abt.

13 August 1942
At 03:30hrs the enemy, supported by tanks, launches a concentrated attack on Julkebino and Jasnaya Poljana, but is halted by our artillery. Our tanks destroy seven enemy tanks in a brief battle. The forward observer of 4.Bttr successfully directs fire on an enemy tank which is destroyed by only two rounds. At 08:00hrs enemy forces, supported by tanks, break through positions near Leushino. A gun from 7.Bttr, providing supporting for the defenders, destroys an enemy tank.

Despite a concentrated barrage by the guns of III.Abt, enemy forces capture Leushino in the evening. After dark the enemy launches a surprise attack with three tanks on Julebino, but two are destroyed by fire from 9.Bttr. Once again in this critical situation the artillerymen held their positions, which encouraged the riflemen to follow.

14 August 1942
In the early dawn, the Soviets launched another attack with tanks on the sector held by

Above:
A temporary bridge constructed by German engineers has collapsed under the considerable weight of an early production SdKfz 7 towing a 15cm *schwere Feldhaubitz* (s FH – heavy field howitzer) 18.

Below:
The entry into service of the 15cm s FH 18, finally gave the German military a truly modern artillery weapon. The gun had good overall performance, but when compared to the Soviet ML-20, which was some 2,540kg heavier, it lacked performance: The Russian gun had a maximum range 17km, whereas the s FH 18 had a maximum range of 13km.

II.Abt. Three heavy tanks were destroyed by artillery fire or mines; the crew of one tank was shot by the VB of 9.Bttr. An assault by following infantry was repelled. At around noon, 17 tanks appeared on our left flank. Immediately the regiment opens fire and the tanks begin to disperse, but were hampered by the boggy terrain; the four which managed to penetrate the frontline were quickly destroyed. The proposed commitment of 1.Bttr as tank destroyer unit is no longer seen as necessary. During the following hours our positions are the target of very heavy fire from enemy mortars, tanks and artillery. Three attempts by the enemy to penetrate Area 3 have been repelled by a concentrated artillery barrage. Our riflemen positioned in this area are enthusiastic about cooperating with the artillery when faced by an enemy attack. Sadly, the area in front of our positions is covered with vast numbers of dead Soviet infantrymen.

As the day progresses, enemy artillery moves its fire to an area near Karmanovo. But our observation battery easily finds the position of the batteries and begins to direct fire.

At 20:00hrs, two enemy tanks with mounted infantry were forced to retreat after being discovered heading north near the supply road.

15 August 1942

At 05:00hrs, the four Russian T-34 tanks open fire on Area 2, but the attack is quickly repelled by fire from I.Abt and III.Abt. In the low ground near Julebino, several enemy tanks become immobilized in the marsh-like terrain. The guns of II.Abt open fire and one tank is hit and catches fire.

The gun commanded by Oberleunant Waetzmann, scores a direct hit on the track of a T-34, destroying it. Unfortunately, Russian troops manage to recover the immobilized tank intact.

At 15:00hrs, the enemy launches a series of artillery attacks on Area 2 and Area 3. As before the guns of I.Abt halt the attacks. The guns of II.Abt positioned in open terrain, begin to bombard the enemy forces, which results heavy losses.

In the evening the enemy increases the pressure: At 18:00hrs he succeeds in breaching our lines near Bttl 'Schwarz', with three T-34 tanks carrying some 80 infantrymen. This forces 4.Bttr to temporarily relocate its B-Stelle (observation post). Two T-34 tanks have been destroyed by our Panzers; another was hit by an 8.8cm FlaK gun.

At around 18.30hrs, the enemy launched another attack on Area 2, but this was quickly halted by concentrated fire from I.Abt and III.Abt. Two enemy tanks are destroyed.

In the period 9 to 15 August, the regiment destroyed a total of 24 enemy tanks and expended 13,481 rounds of ammunition.

Below:
Advancing across Russia was not without its dangers, particularly when relying on the local infrastructure; many of the wooden bridges would have been built by local labour. Here the half-track tractor has crossed safely, but the bridge has failed under the weight (5,487kg) of the 15cm s FH 18. Without the availability of a heavy crane, recovery would be a difficult operation.

PIONEER-BATTALION (MOT)

For centuries pioneers (field engineers) have been of vital importance to many armies. Often underestimated, their true value increased when the first tank appeared and warfare became mechanized, and the scope of missions undertaken by the field engineers became more numerous and hazardous.

A German manual stated that basic engineer training had to be taught in every unit, that a soldier must be able to carry out simple tasks such as cutting through barbed-wire defences and using a bayonet to locate mines laid by an enemy.

Dedicated pioneer units had to perform difficult tasks with what equipment was to hand and they would be forced to improvise.

Panzer-Pioniere (armoured engineers) were assigned missions which emerged during the advance; many were carried out ahead of the frontline.

As the Panzer divisions were being established, the planning for the creation of specialized armoured engineer units began. But the first units did not join the Panzer division until early in 1940.

Even the establishment of (conventional) infantry engineer platoons could not be completed despite an urgent requirement. In January 1940, *Oberkommando des Heeres* (OKH – high command of the army) urged for units to be formed for more than 50 infantry regiments: The *Blitzkrieg* on Western Europe was only a few months away.

At the same time the Panzer divisions continued to wait. In January 1940, the high command of 106th Army Corps demanded that the establishment of engineer units for the Panzer divisions be accelerated:

> The inability of the engineers, in their original form, to closely follow the advance of our Panzer or *Schützen* (gep) was demonstrated during the Polish campaign.
>
> We have repeatedly emphasized the great importance of engineers for combat by the Panzer division. Unfavourable terrain, stronger defences, better-prepared, better-equipped and better-led enemy [French] forces underline our demand for the best possible cooperation. This task can only be provided under the protection of armour. The armoured engineer battalion must be issued with tanks, furthermore the soonest delivery of armoured personnel carriers is desirable.

In March 1940, the OKH ordered the establishment of *Panzerpionier-Kompanien* (PzPiKp) for the PzPiBtl of 1.PzDiv, 2.PzDiv, 3.PzDiv, 4.PzDiv, and 10.PzDiv by a reorganization of their existing companies. The following, 5.PzDiv, 6.PzDiv, 7.PzDiv, 8.PzDiv and 9.PzDiv would receive new establishments.

Far left:
The *Flammpanzer* (flame-thrower tank) was initially issued to independent battalions at army troop level. The first of the type were based on the PzKpfw II and were not successful. In 1943, the equipment was installed in the PzKpfw III which was a success. In service the type was issued to specialized *Flammzüge* (flamethrower platoon) incorporated in the staff company of the armoured battalion.

Left:
Bridging water obstacles was the prime task for pioneer units. A *Brückengerät* Type C (capacity 2,030kg) is being constructed over a number of pontoon ferries. As work continues, a bicycle troop is being ferried across in *Flosssäcke* (inflatable dinghies).

Above:
A PzBefWg III crosses a partially destroyed cast-concrete bridge. Pioneers have attempted to fill the gap with debris and *Übergangsschienen* (bridging sections). An SdKfz 7/1, mounting a 2cm FlaK-Vierling 38, has been positioned to provide anti-aircraft cover.

The reorganization and the establishment of the 3.PzPiKp (within the PiBtl [mot]) would be accomplished by the end of March. But, due to a shortage of equipment the deadline could not be met.

The PiBtl (mot) had the following structure:

Bataillonstab – battalion HQ
two *le Pionierkompanien* – light pioneer company
one *Panzerpionierkompanie* – armoured pioneer company
one *Brückenkolonne* B (mot) – bridge column B (motorized)
one or two *Brückenkolonne* K (mot) – bridge column K (motorized)
Kolonne (mot) einer PzDiv – transport column

Headquarters section

The *Gruppe Führer* (HQ section), to KStN 703, was equipped with three motorcycles, two combinations and three Kfz 15. The *Nachrichten-Staffel* (signals section) was issued with a Kfz 2 and a Kfz 15 also a light truck. The

section had two TornFuTrp 'b' portable radio squads and two TornFuTrp 'b' (mot) issued with light and medium cross-country cars. A telephone section carried 1,000m field telephone cable.

The *Gefechtstross* I (combat train) was issued with a motorcycle and also a light truck carrying a field kitchen. The *Gefechtstross* II had a combination, a Kfz 15 and also two 3-ton trucks and 4.5-ton truck. A Kfz 31 ambulance could be included, but it was usually in the main column.

Light armoured engineer company

The *Gruppe Führer* (HQ section) for the *leichte Pionierkompanie* (light armoured engineer company), to KStN 714, was supplied with two motorcycles and two combinations, a Kfz 15 and two light trucks.

The *Nachrichten-Staffel* (signals section) was supplied with two TornFuTrp 'b' (mot) carried in the Kfz 15.

The *Zugtrupp* (HQ section) was issued with a motorcycle, a combination, a Kfz 15 and 3-ton truck. The *Pionierzug* (engineer platoons) were formed

Above:
Bridging sections were often utilized to assemble a temporary ferry. Load capacity can only be estimated, but a SdKfz 10 and a 3.7cm PaK do not appear to cause any problems.

Right:
Elements of 1.PzDiv use this *Brückengerät* Type B to cross the river Meuse during the invasion of France. The bridge had a span of 50m, and a maximum capacity of 24,390kg, sufficient for all German tanks at the time. This *Sanitätspanzer* I (ambulance tank) was modified by the workshop engineers of 1.PzDiv and uses a *Fahrschulwanne* (driving instruction chassis).

as three sections, each provided with a motorcycle, a combination, two light cross-country cars and five light trucks.

The *Gefechtstross* (combat train) was issued with a light truck, two 3-ton trucks and a *Feldküche* (field kitchen).

The *Gepäckstross* and *Verpflegungstross* were issued with a motorcycle and two light trucks. A support section transported material (wood) in five heavy trucks. Furthermore a motorcycle and a le Pkw was available.

The engineer transport company carried great variety of engineer equipment, including rubber dinghies, air compressors, 1,000kg of explosives (different charges), smoke flares and reels of barbed wire.

Armoured engineers

The *Panzerpionier-Kompanie* (armoured engineer company), to KStN 716, was the most important and well-equipped part of the battalion.

The *Gruppe Führer* (HQ section) was supplied with two motorcycles, a combination and a Kfz 15. The unit also had a PzKpfw I and a PzKpfw II.

Demolition

The first and second platoons were designated *Zerstörungszug* (demolition platoons). Both were issued with five PzKpfw I and a light truck. The PzKpfw I were fitted with a crane-type frame with a container to carry a large explosive device. The tank would be driven in reverse gear up an obstacle; the charge was then lowered into position and the tank driven away. After a short delay, the charge would detonate and destroy the obstacle.

Although no specific information has at yet been found, it appears most likely that engineer units received the tanks and fabricated and fitted the frames in the workshops.

Apparently the 'Zerstörer' did not prove to be effective. The modified PzKpfw I and some PzKpfw II so modified were driven in reverse up to the target. The thin armour at the rear of both types only protected against machine gun fire; an anti-tank rifle or armour-piercing bullets would easily immobilize such a slow-moving target.

Bridgelayers

The 3.(*Brückenleger*) *Kompanie* (bridgelayer company), was issued with twenty PzKpfw IV hulls modified to carry a 9m folding bridge. Being armoured the type was capable of being operated in combat conditions very close to the battlefront. The bridging sections could be used individually (it was also possible to use a single span) to replace a destroyed bridge or to cross many types of obstacle. The commander of each platoon was issued with a PzKpfw II and four *Brückenleger* IV.

The vehicles were operated by PiBtl (mot) and supported 1.PzDiv, 2.PzDiv, 3.PzDiv, 5.PzDiv and 10.PzDiv.

Left:
Pioneers had to deal with many problems when assembling a bridge including strong currents. Here a *Brückengerät* Type B has been laid over pontoons, each of which has strong mooring lines attached to the river bank.

The units operating the type identified a number of problems: The running wheels were subjected to excessive wear, the road speed was considered to be too slow and the range was only 40km when carrying the bridge-laying equipment.

After the fall of France, 16 *Brückenleger* IV were taken back to Germany, dismantled and rebuilt as a PzKpfw IV.

Four of the type remained in service, but without the bridging equipment. This was removed and replaced with an extending (fire brigade type) turntable ladder. The type became known as the *Sturmstegpanzer* (assault ladder tank) and was used by infantry to cross gaps or to climb obstacles. A number of these vehicles were used during the initial phases of *Unternehmen* Barbarossa. A number of after-action reports indicate that the *Sturmstegpanzer* was deployed with much success.

Although research and development continued, Germany did not produce an improved version of the bridge-layer tank. This is somewhat understandable since the German armaments industry was not producing sufficient tanks to meet with demand.

It was intended to issue the fourth platoon of each PzPiKp with six SdKfz 251/5 *Pionier-Schützenpanzerwagen* (assault engineer vehicle), to

Below:
Pioneer units were issued with the SdKfz 251/7 *Pionier-Gerätewagen* (engineer equipment carrier) which carried two *Übergangsschienen* (bridging sections). Specialist equipment including explosives were transported inside the vehicle.

carry men and their equipment. But again unavailability due to production problems forced the units to use standard issue 3-ton trucks.

There were a number of PzKpfw I and PzKpfw II tanks adapted to carry some form of bridging equipment. But little information exists as to the type of equipment fitted and the number produced is unknown.

Above:
A PzKpfw I of 2.PzDiv about to be ferried across a wide river stream; a *Brückengerät* Type B has been used to assemble a pontoon ferry which is powered by two large outboard motors.

Bridging equipment

Military planners decided that each division (infantry, motorized infantry and tank) would be issued with bridging equipment. Normally they meant pontoon bridges, which could be assembled to span even the widest river. Before the war, a large number of *Brückengerät* (BruGer – bridging equipment) types (A, B, C, D, G, K and J) for many different applications had been designed. The development continued as heavier tanks such as the PzKpfw V Panther entered service.

Virtually all Panzer divisions were issued with BrüGer B and most also had one or two BrüGer K.

Above:
Elements of 1.PzDiv cross a canal during the invasion of France. The *Brückengerät* Type B was an effective and reliable piece of equipment for all mobile units, including a tank division.

Right:
In early 1940, the pioneer battalion in a Panzer division began to be issued with specialized bridge-laying vehicles. The PzKpfw II, one of the more improvised types, was fitted with simple ramps to bridge obstacles.

Left:
During the invasion of Poland, pioneer units used the PzKpfw I to transport heavy baulks of timber and prefabricated bridging sections.

Below:
A temporary crossing has been laid by a *Brückenleger* IV c armoured bridge-laying vehicle. The PzKpfw III is towing a trailer carrying two 200-litre drums of fuel.

Bridge type B

The *Brückengerät* B (bridging equipment), to KStN 733, was the standard type issued to all combat engineer battalions. When assembled a BruGer B had a maximum span of 83m and maximum load capacity of some 8,100kg. A BruGer built to span 57m had a maximum load capacity of some 20,300kg. If the pontoon bridge was built to span 50m then the load capacity could be increased to the maximum; 24,400kg. This was important since the PzKpfw IV (also the *Sturmgeschütz*) exceeded the maximum load capacity.

A large amount of equipment (and men) was required to assemble this type of bridge:

48 pontoons transported on 16 special trailers.
Eight trestles transported on four trailers.
Six *Sturmboote* (assault boats) and two M-*Boote*

The equipment was divided between two platoons. Half-track tractors, normally the SdKfz 6, were provided if the pontoon trailers had to be moved over rough terrain. Heavy trucks would be used to haul the trailers carrying the trestles.

Below:
Some 20 *Brückenleger* IV were completed before the invasion of France. Each bridge section was designed to span a gap of approximately 8m. But the type suffered from constant mechanical problems due to it weighing 30,480kg, much too heavy for the transmission and running gear of the PzKpfw IV chassis.

Above:
Clearing and laying mines was everyday business for pioneer troops. This soldier 'armed' with rifle and a flexible probe has been successful in his search and detection of mine.

A truck-mounted support platoon carried all other equipment required to assemble the bridge including, hawsers, winches and ramps.

Bridge type K

The pontoon bridge type K was almost identical in capacity to the type B, but was assembled using 24 pontoons. The BruGer K had a standard capacity of 20,300kg when built to its maximum span of 77m. As with the BruGer B, capacity could be increased to 24,400kg if the span was reduced. The BrüGer K was only issued to PzDiv, *Panzerkorps* and InfDiv (mot).

Note: In 1940 when the unit was established, it was known as the *Pionier-Battailon* (mot). The term *Panzerpionier-Battailon* (PzPioAbt – armoured engineer battalion) was first used for the invasion of Russia. When Guderian took command of the *Panzertruppen* and issued the PzDiv 43 structure, *Panzerpionier-Battalion* would be the only title used for the force.

Right:
Members of pioneer unit
mount a PzKpfw IV Ausf D
of the *Panzerarmee Afrika*;
note the soldier next to
the tank commander is
carrying a *Flammenwerfer*
(flamethrower) 34 on his
back.(Getty)

The recovery of wounded personnel from the battlefield was essential for all military formations including a Panzer division. Medics often had work under fire, but lacked the protection of specialized, highly mobile armoured motor vehicles. This further hindered the evacuation of casualties.

In August 1940, the medical officer of 10.PzDiv sent a report detailing the lack of organization during the French campaign.

The division is critical of the decision to organize the two medical companies according to SanKp 'a' (mot) standard. In contrast to the initial provision, the type 'a' was divided in two platoons, alternating their deployments, to operate constant and effective medical services. The quality and strength of the medical company was considered sufficient, but considered two surgeons to be insufficient and requested that this be increased to four.

Initially, the Panzer division was not issued with a military hospital. However, those officers responsible claimed that it should be treated with the same as an infantry division. But this would require the loss of one of the two medical companies.

The three ambulance platoons were each issued with ten vehicles: six more than authorized.

All divisional units – the Panzer battalion, the rifle battalion, the pioneer-battalion

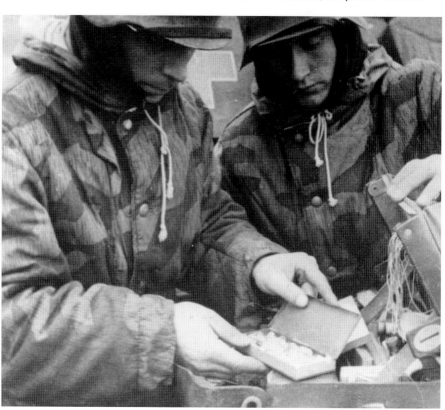

Right:
Two German medical orderlies examine a box of field dressings and simple medical equipment. The SdKfz 251/8 *Krankenpanzerwagen* (armoured ambulance) was used to recover wounded from the battlefield and deliver them to a treatment centre.

Left:
A SdKfz 251/1 mounted with a
2.8cm *schwere Panzerbüchse*
(s PzB – heavy anti-tank
rifle) 41. The gun had an
effective range of 300m
against enemy armour and
in 1941 it was regarded as
being superior to the 3.7cm
PaK when firing tungsten
rounds. The s PzB also
fired high-explosive (HE)
rounds for combat against
soft-skinned targets,
machine-gun positions and
buildings. The vehicle is in
service with an unidentified
SS unit.

Above:
The SdKfz 251/8 armoured ambulance was equipped with a large tarpaulin to cover the open bodywork and protect the wounded from the Russian weather. Casualties would be taken to a *Hauptverbandsplatz* (dressing section) for assessment. Seriously wounded personnel would be moved onward to a *Feldlazarett* (field hospital) for surgery, often in a horse-drawn ambulance.

and the reconnaissance battalion – were normally issued with one ambulance. But experience in combat has shown that this was considerably inadequate: Accordingly 10.PzDiv urgently requests that this be increased to two instead. During combat, the division was forced to use ambulances captured from the enemy to make up for the shortage.

Unfortunately an armoured ambulance was not yet available, although delivery of type was planned by the ordnance department. However, the Panzer regiment decided to use a number of standard SdKfz 251, commandeered from the rifle regiment, as ambulances. These vehicles, although not correctly equipped, performed effectively on the battlefield. Therefore it is urgently requested that each regiment is supplied with four specialized armoured ambulances.

In 1942, these versatile and effective vehicles began to be delivered to front-line units. But delivery was slow due to production problems in Germany.

In June 1942, I./SchRgt 126 of 23.PzDiv submitted an after-action report:

Tactical deployment
Organization
The battalion was usually exclusively deployed as an essential element of a combat group.
2. Tactical missions
During an attack, the battalion was always included in the second or third wave; a tactic used commonly by a light tank battalion rather than that of a conventional rifle battalion.

However, poor ground conditions and heavy enemy fire forced the un-armoured elements to follow the battle. Thus, it is essential that all medical units are equipped with a sufficient number of half-track armoured ambulances. But it should be remembered that when the *Schützenpanzerwagen* [SPw – armoured personnel carrier] is deployed in close cooperation with tanks it is never used to lead the attack, since the enemy is aware that the SPw has thin armour and attacks it with concentrated fire when spotted.

6. Attending of injured

The battalion requires at least one armoured ambulance, as issued to a Panzer regiment. In combat, the battalion deployed one armoured ambulance which followed the attack; this allowed battle casualties to receive effective treatment or rapidly evacuated to a field hospital. All *Sanitäts-Kraftwagen* [Sanka – soft-skinned ambulance] in the unit did not follow the attack.

8. General issues

On a number of occasions, senior officers ordered that armoured half-track vehicles were to be used to transport ammunition and rations. To do so, weapons and equipment had to be removed, which resulted in a weakening of the combat ability.

Below:
On 26 December 1944, Soviet forces achieved the encirclement of Budapest trapping the Hungarian and German defenders. On 11 February 1945, an evacuation of the city began as civilians and military personnel moved to the north, but on 13 February the German commander defied Hitler and ordered the surrender. Here a number of German troops have boarded an SdKfz 251/8, armoured ambulance; the vehicle was not equipped with a machine gun, and only carried light infantry weapons.

CHAPTER 6

ANCILLARY UNITS

A military unit as large and as fast moving as a Panzer division can only operate effectively if it is supported by an efficient supply (logistics) system.

Training manoeuvres before the war had identified weaknesses in the supply system. Soon after the outbreak of war this became a reality. For instance, if a unit ran out of ammunition it would be forced to 'borrow' from one that had a surplus until it was replenished. Food was important for the health and morale of the troops and shortages would be made up by purchasing, or more likely, commandeering supplies from various sources in an occupied area. In dire circumstances a transport horse would be slaughtered for fresh meat.

All logistic requirements would be transported from manufacturers to be warehoused at military depots in Germany; later in occupied countries. From these units the army, working in close cooperation with the *Reichsbahn* (German national railways), would oversee the transport to the required destination. Once again, the material would be stored at main depots.

The army supply organization would then distribute the material to a number of smaller army depots near to where the division was deployed. Transport from the division would then be used to deliver the supplies to forces fighting (or advancing) on the frontline.

During the short Polish campaign the lines of supply worked reasonably well; any problems, errors and shortcomings were quickly realized and remedied.

Although the launch of *Unternehmen* (Operation) Barbarossa began with German forces making rapid progress into Soviet territory, the weather

Far left:
As German forces advanced across northern Europe in 1940, a large number of industrial buildings were captured intact and many would be used for storage or as maintenance and repair facilities by workshop units. Here various light vehicles, trucks and an SdKfz 10/4 are being worked on by engineers.

would take its toll. Supply units would be challenged by problems, often difficult to solve. The majority of roads were unpaved and the network was almost non-existent: many were simple cart tracks between villages and towns. During the hot and dry summer, the cooling radiators on many vehicles became blocked by the ever-present clouds of thick dust. Heavy showers during the summer and the constant rain in autumn turned many tracks into bottomless mud, making them impassable. As the Russian winter arrived the mud first turned to slush then to deep frozen ruts. The extremely low temperatures brought with them further troubles, when engines and transmissions froze. Heavy falls of snow stopped any movement, even by fully tracked vehicles. The resupply of ammunition and other vital supplies became almost impossible.

The Russian rail network was built using a number of different track gauges which forced the Germans invader to utilize Russian-built locomotives and rolling stock. A constant source of delays and the destruction of consignments were the many attacks by Russian partisan forces. The now better-equipped Soviet air force also began carrying out attacks.

Below:
In 1939, the *Luftwaffe* had some 550 Junkers Ju-52 transports in service. The aircraft, which could operate from unprepared surfaces, had an economic cruising speed of 209kph and a range of 998km. By 1944, a total of some 2,800 had been delivered to the *Luftwaffe*.

Above:
In 1941, the severe winter in Russia brought the German invasion to a halt. Vehicles failed or could not operate in the deep snow. This required front-line troops to improvise and use horse-drawn sledges to transport supplies through the deep snow and frozen slush.

Divisional logistics

In 1939 it was planned for a Panzer division to have a complement of some 13,000 personnel: 394 officers, 115 civilian officials, 1,963 NCOs and 9,321 conscripts. These men had to be clothed, accommodated, fed and cared for medically. The tanks, other heavy equipment and vehicles in the unit required fuel and spare parts; the weapons ammunition.

For all these services the Panzer division was provided with a specialist unit; the *Nachschub-Bataillon* (supply battalion). This unit was responsible for the supply of everything from paperclips to anti-tank ammunition. It was led by the *Divisions-Nachschubführer* (divisional supply commander), and was made up as follows::

Seven *kleine Kraftwagenkolonne* (light transport columns).

Three *große Kraftwagenkolonne – betriebsstoff* (heavy transport columns – fuel).

Two *Panzer-Werkstattkompanie* (tank repair/maintenance company).

One *Nachschub-Kompanie* (supply company).
Two *Sanitäts-Kompanie* 'b' (first-aid company).
One *Krankenkraftwagen-Kompanie* (ambulance company).
One *Feldgendarmerie Trupp* (military police section).
One *Feldpostamt* (mot) (post office [motorized]).
One *Verpflegungsamt* (rations office).
One *Schlächterei-Zug* (butchers' platoon).
One *Bäckerei-Kompanie* 'e' (bakery company).

Supply battalion

The *Stab Division* (HQ section) of a *Nachsrub-Bataillon* (supply battalion), to KStN 1208, was a relatively small unit, which worked very closely with the *Verpflegungsamt* (rations office, see below). The HQ commander was issued with a medium car, and the unit was equipped with a light truck and a passenger-type coach.

Left:
On the North African battlefield all supplies had to be transported over long distances. The *Afrika Korps* utilized all types of load-carrying vehicle including those captured from British and Commonwealth forces: A Bedford MWD forms part of the convoy. (Getty)

Transport column

Seven *kleine Kraftwagenkolonne* (light light transport column), to KStN 1225, each with a cargo capacity of 30,480kg were available to carry supplies and equipment. Each column had a section from HQ which was issued with a motorcycle, a combination and two Kfz 2 light cars. A support section was supplied with a combination and a light truck.

Heavy transport column (fuel)

Three *große Kraftwagenkolonne (betriebsstoff)* heavy transport column (fuel), to KStN 1226, were equipped with three heavy trucks. In the German army it was standard practice to use refillable 200-litre drums or 20-litre 'Jerrycans' to carry fuel, and transport them on a standard heavy truck. The HQ section was issued with a motorcycle, a combination and a Kfz 2 light car. The support section was equipped with a combination and a light truck.

Right:
Two Henschel *Typ* 33 trucks
pass through a road block
during the invasion of
France. Both are towing a
steel-bodied two-axle Hf 7
Stahlfeldwagen trailer; the
type usually hauled by a
team of horses.

Supply company (motorized)

The *Nachschub-Kompanie* (mot), (supply company [motorized]), to KStN 1255, was responsible for loading the correct supplies and the unloading of the trucks at their destination. While the trucks were being unloaded, the drivers were expected to maintain their vehicles. The HQ section was issued with two combinations, a light car and a light truck. The three supply platoons and a workshop platoon were issued with a motorcycle and three medium trucks each. The transport support section was provided with a motorcycle and a light truck.

Below:
Once a frontline had been established a number of supply points would be opened to allow troops to purchase tobacco, cigarettes and other goods.

Above:
Summer 1941: Four German soldiers appear to be enjoying a delivery of beer during the early phase of *Unternehmen* Barbarossa. They wear a mesh-type cloth on their heads as protection against the constant 'plague' of flies.

Left:
A French-built van fitted out as a mobile office for *Kriegsberichtschreibe* (war report writers) who followed events on the battlefront for the news media in the Fatherland.

Left:
A Panzer division needed
to be constantly supplied
with not only food, fuel and
ammunition but also spare
parts and replacement
troops. A convoy of trucks
which includes a large number
of French-built Renault AH
ascends a mountain road in
Libya. Note all the vehicles
carry identification markings
or flags to prevent attack by
patrolling *Luftwaffe* aircraft.
British Commonwealth forces
have abandoned a Cruiser Tank
A10, a Daimler Dingo armoured
scout car and a Standard 8
staff car as they made their
retreat. (Getty)

Right:
The Nazi regime thrived
on bureaucracy and even
the military had to keep
accurate records. Here a
company clerk brings a
unit's records up to date
during a lull in the fighting.

Left:
A Horch Kfz 12 receiving petrol from 200-litre drums at a refuelling point as a clerk prepares and stamps the always-required paperwork. All tactical markings on the vehicle have been obliterated: common practice by propaganda units.

Left:
The 25-litre Jerrycan was an effective way of transporting fuel. The *Wehrmacht-Einheitskanister* (army standard canister) was painted green, but a white cross would be applied to indicate that it was to be used only for water.

Left:
A captured Leyland Retriever recovery gantry vehicle being used by German engineers as they lift the turret from an SdKfz 223. Note the vehicle has received a German cross, the letters WH (*Wehrmacht Heer*) and a tactical mark. (SZ Photo)

Right:
German workshop units were issued with the 20-ton capacity *Sonderanhänger* (SdAnh – flat-bed trailer) 116. For recovery duties it would usually be hauled by an SdKfz 9, heavy half-track tractor; a combination that proved very effective, but only over firm terrain.

Right:
Two 300-litre fuel drums positioned on the cargo bed of a standard 3-ton truck fitted with a simple hand pump. Vehicles could be filled directly or the fuel would be pumped into Jerrycans for distribution.

Left:
When the PzKpfw V Panther medium and PzKpfw VI Tiger heavy tank entered service many workshop units had to be re-equipped. Beside powerful heavy recovery vehicles they were also issued with a gantry crane to lift heavy items such as a complete turret assembly. The units would be positioned some distance from the frontline, out of range to enemy artillery and well concealed from enemy air activity.

Right:
An engineer, assisted by the tank commander, works on a mechanical problem with a PzKpfw IV, Ausf A in service with Panzer-Lehr-Regiment. His tools and other equipment are carried in a Stöwer-built Kfz 2/40 *Instandsetzungs-Kraftwagen* (workshop car).

Workshop company (mot)

Each supply battalion was assigned two *Werkstatt-Kompanie* (workshop company), to KStN 1052. The HQ section was issued with a motorcycle and a Kfz 2. Each of the two maintenance platoons was issued with a combination, a light car, a light truck, a medium truck, a passenger-type coach, and a Kfz 79 *werkstatt-kraftwagen* (workshop truck: covered). They were also equipped with an SdKfz 7 half-track tractor and two trailers to carry tools and spare parts. The *waffenmeister-zug* (armourer platoon) was issued with two combinations, a light truck and four medium trucks. The combat, rations and supply trains were provided with a combination, a Kfz 2 and two light trucks.

Left:
Engineers at a commandeered facility in France use a portable gantry-type crane to lift the engine from an SdKfz 10. One of the many Bedford MWD light trucks captured from British forces is in the background. Both vehicles are in service with 1.PzDiv.

Below:
Workshop personnel were often forced to improvise in the field. Here two engineers have utilized two fuel drums and some lengths of timber to assemble a simple workbench.

Field hospital

The divisional *Armsarzt* (medical officer) commanded two medical companies and an ambulance company which formed a *Feldlazarett* (field hospital), to KStN 1342.

The unit was responsible for setting up a tented *Hauptverbandsplatz* (clearing station) which included an assessment facility, surgical operating theatre and recovery areas. The hospital would be erected some 4km to 8km to the rear of the frontline; where possible an intact building would be utilized. The staff section was issued with two combinations, a light truck and a medium passenger-type coach. The two *Lazarett-Zug* (hospital platoons) were provided with a light car, three light trucks and a medium truck, and a light passenger-type coach. Each also had a Kfz 31 *Krankenwagen* (ambulance).

Below:
A number of 'wounded' soldiers being unloaded from a Phänomen-built Kfz 31 ambulance during an exercise.

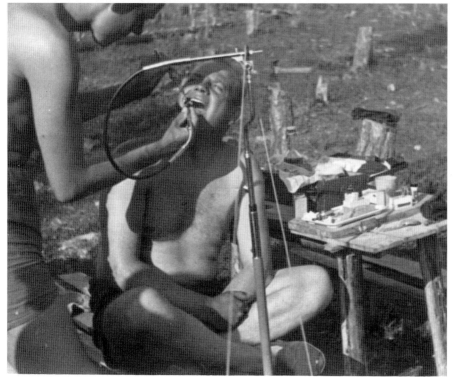

Above:
A tented *Feldlazarett* (field hospital), where the wounded would be assessed and receive basic life-saving treatment, has been positioned in a shallow depression. Unfortunately these often large encampments were difficult to camouflage and were subject to artillery and air attack.

Left:
The doctors and other medical staff of a field hospital had to deal with wide variety of ailments. Here a dental surgeon is drilling a tooth cavity; fortunately the patient would have received a local anaesthetic and the equipment is electrically driven.

Ambulance company

A *Krankenkraftwagen-Kompanie* ambulance company, to KStN 1365, was responsible for the recovery and also the evacuation of wounded personnel. The HQ section was issued with a light car and two light trucks. The unit was formed as three platoons issued with a total of 15 Kfz 31 ambulances.

Right:
A Ford V8 *Maultier* (mule) fitted with cabin-type bodywork as a Kfz 305/76 *Sanitätsgerätkraftwagen* (medical equipment vehicle).

Right:
The *mittlerer Kraftomnibus* (m KOM – medium passenger bus) was often used by medical units. This vehicle, built on a Ford G 917 chassis, has been painted white with conspicuous red crosses. The type could only be on used hard-surfaced tracks or roads.

Above:
An Austin K2 ambulance in service with a German medical unit; the vehicle is one of the many abandoned by British forces as they retreated from France.

Next page:
The Ju-52/3mg7e was an improved version of the versatile aircraft. It was fitted with larger cargo doors to improve access and could carry 12 stretcher cases or 18 troops. During the siege of Stalingrad, the type was used to evacuate the seriously wounded from the battlefront. (Getty)

Medical companies

The two *Sanitätskompanie* (medical companies), to KStN 1313, were responsible for a large number of duties and were supported by mobile surgery sections. Their HQ was better equipped, being issued with two motorcycles, two Kfz 15 cross-country cars, a light truck and a passenger-type coach. It was also issued with two kl FuTrp 'a' (light radio) sections. The two *Sanitäts-Zug* (medical platoons), were each equipped with a combination, a Kfz 11, five medium trucks, and a truck with an enclosed body. The unit also had five Kfz 31 ambulances.

Below:
A field medic bandages the wounds of a *Kradschützen* (motorcycle riflemen) from 1.PzDiv before he is transported to the first-aid station for further treatment.

Above:
Phänomen Werke Gustav Hiller was the most prolific supplier of the Kfz 31 *Krankenkraftwagen* (ambulance) which the company built on the *Granit* (granite) 25 light truck chassis at their facility in Zittau. It could transport four stretcher cases.

Left:
The Fieseler Fi 156 *Storch* (stork) D-1 was the air-ambulance version of the specialist aircraft. The machine, which had a stalling speed of 46kph, could land in 20m and take-off in 50m.

Butchery section

The staff section of the *Schlächterei-Kompanie* (mot) (butchery company [motorized]), was provided with a motorcycle, a combination and a light car. The two platoons were issued with a total of six medium trucks, two trailers and also power generators. The train section had one combination, one light car and three light trucks.

The small HQ section of the *Schlächterei-Zug* (butchery platoon), to KStN 1282, was issued with two motorcycles and a light car. The unit was formed as two platoons issued with six medium trucks and two power generators. The train section was provided with a combination, a light car and three light trucks.

Below:
Often the rapid advance made by a Panzer division forced ancillary units to improvise. Here butchers have set up an open-air abattoir to slaughter animals and process the carcasses for cooking. Each soldier would receive a daily ration of 136g of meat including bones.

Above:
When in combat, German troops seized every opportunity to acquire (or steal) fresh meat. Here a pig has been slaughtered and is ready to be cut into joints for cooking.

Left:
German front-line forces were fed according to a daily *Verpflegungssplatz* (meal plan) Rations 1, which included rye bread, meat, vegetables, pulses and fish, altogether weighing approximately 1.7kg. (SZ Photo)

Bakery section

The HQ section of the *Bäckerei-Kompanie* (mot) (bakery company [motorized]), to KStN 1277, was equipped with a motorcycle and a light car. The section was formed as two platoons and each was issued with three heavy trucks and a medium passenger-type coach. It also had three trailers: one carried a dough mixer and two each which carried the bread ovens. The train section was supplied with a combination, a light car and three light trucks.

Right:
A number of SdAnh 106 *Backanhänger* (bakery trailer) of a field bakery company: the logistics for such an operation were formidable since the daily allowance for each man in combat was 700g of rye bread.

Right:
Men from a field bakery using a Russian-built Komsomoletz tractor captured from the Red Army to tow an SdKfz 106 bakery trailer and a *Feldküche* (field kitchen).

Left:
To produce dough, the bakery company was equipped with the SdAnh 36 *Teigknetmaschine* (dough mixer) and also a truck-mounted water tank. Power was supplied by a 0.5Kw *Maschinensatz* (generator). (SZ Photo)

Field kitchen

Good nutrition was, and still is, essential to maintain the health and morale of all combat units. In many previous campaigns the lack of sufficient food had often affected the ability and willingness of troops to fight on the battlefront. As rations were consumed replenishments had to be purchased from the people in occupied countries, but most often supplies were commandeered, pillaged or looted.

In 1910, German armed forces began to be issued with mobile cooking facilities. The *Feldküchen* (field kitchens) consisted of two wagons; one to carry food, the other mounted with an oven, kitchen tools and fuel. Normally the kitchens would be hauled by a team of two or four horses.

The same equipment remained in service throughout World War II. For motorized units, the oven was mounted on a heavy cross-country vehicle or truck. Any similar equipment captured from the enemy was, whenever possible, utilized to prepare food: German troops soon named these kitchens '*Gulaschkanone*' (goulash cannon).

Right:
The *Feldküche* (field kitchen) first entered service in World War I and continued, virtually unchanged, in use throughout World War II. It could be hauled by two horses, but it was usual practice to use a team of four. (SZ Photo)

Above:
For troops in the field, rations would be collected from a field kitchen and then delivered to their position. To keep the food hot and fresh, it would be packed in insulated containers. (SZ Photo)

Water supply

As German forces advanced across mainland Europe they never experienced a shortage of water. Many of the regions already had an established fresh-water system; otherwise there was an abundance of fresh-water lakes, rivers and streams from which to draw supplies.

But in the deserts of North Africa the supply situation was completely different, since water was hard to come by and had to be collected from an oasis, a wadi or a well dug by locals.

To bolster supplies, water was also drawn from the sea and passed through a diesel-powered mobile desalination plant, assembled and operated by pioneers, to produce salt-free water.

Whatever the source, the water would be sent to a distribution point where it would be put into 'Jerrycans' or 200-litre drums for delivery to front-line forces.

Below:
In the deserts of North Africa, a reliable and regular supply of water was essential for survival. Water could not only be sourced from an oasis, a wadi or a local well, but also from the sea. Here engineers are assembling a mobile desalination plant to produce salt-free water. (Getty)

Above:
Like fuel, drinking water could also be transported in 20-litre *Wehrmacht-Einheitskanister* (army standard containers) which Allied forces called the 'Jerrycan' – 'Jerry' being the slang for a German. Those for carrying water were marked with a prominent white cross. (SZ Photo)

Left:
Water from the desalination plant was piped to a distribution manifold and then to filling stations. (Getty)

Field postal

The *Feldpostamt* (field post section) was a motorized unit, to KStN 2251, equipped with three light cars and a medium truck. The unit was responsible for collecting and delivering post for the fighting troops.

Above:
Many Soviet prisoners of war or civilians 'volunteered' to work for the *Wehrmacht*. Known as *Hilfswillige* (Hiwis – helpers) they were used for a variety tasks, including delivering letters and parcels.

Military police

A *Feldgendarmerie* (military police) section, to KStN 2033b, was responsible not only for maintaining discipline, but also directing traffic as territory was gained or lost. The section was usually equipped with four combinations, 14 light cars and a light truck.

Right:
The German *Feldgendarmerie* (field police) was established during the Napoleonic wars. All men recruited to the service were also fully trained for infantry warfare. Here a *Feldgendarm* has been assigned to direct traffic in a town in the grip of a Russian winter.
(SZ Photo)

Left:
Three *Feldgendarmen*, also known as *Kettenhunde* (watchdog), fix a direction sign to a wall in a village near Sedan after German forces had crossed the border of France in 1940. The gorget (a decorative plate worn at the neck) was a distinctive part of the uniform. (SZ Photo)

Below:
Feldgendarmerie operating as infantry follow a BT-5 light cavalry tank, captured intact from the Red Army, to launch an attack on a position held by Russian partisan forces. (SZ Photo)

Left:
A bomb from an enemy aircraft has exploded close to a group of German vehicles. The truck is a British-built Bedford OYD, one of the many captured from British forces as they retreated from France in 1940.

Right:
The Panzer division was a self-contained unit which even had its own shoemaker. (Getty)

INDEX

1.PzDiv 8, 10, 14, 26, 34, 57, 69–70, 72, 76–7, 83, 98–9, 104–5, 108, 119, 152, 155, 170, 175, 183, 217, 222–3, 257, 264
basic original structure for 26
2.PzDiv 13, 69, 80, 83, 99, 104, 121, 125, 147, 152, 155, 210, 217, 223, 225
4.PzDiv 51, 69, 86, 99, 104, 152, 155, 217
3.PzDiv 33, 69, 83, 87, 99, 101, 104, 111, 149, 151–2, 155, 217, 223–4
5.PzDiv 70, 99, 104, 155, 199, 217, 223
6.PzDiv 59, 61–2, 71, 87, 96, 98–9, 104–5, 108, 152, 155, 158, 185, 217
7.PzDiv 15, 17, 69, 71, 83, 94, 98–9, 104, 152, 155, 173, 215
8.PzDiv 71, 98–9, 104, 152, 155, 181, 217
9.PzDiv 54, 99, 104, 152, 155, 217
10.PzDiv 7, 70, 99, 104, 144, 149, 152, 155, 217, 223, 232, 234
11.PzDiv 152
12.PzDiv 42, 152
13.PzDiv 151–2
14.PzDiv 152
15.PzDiv 65, 189
16.PzDiv 152
17.PzDiv 152
18.PzDiv 152, 181
19.PzDiv 152
20.PzDiv 152
23.PzDiv 111, 234
1.SS-PzDiv Leibstandarte-SS Adolf Hitler (LSSAH) 152
2.SS-PzDiv Das Reich (DR) 152
3.SS-PzDiv Totenkopf 152

Adler *Typ* 10N 40
Artillerie-Regiment 175
Aufklärung-Abteilung (reconnaissance battalion) 17
Aufklärungskörper (reconnaissance corps) 121
Austin K2 261

Barbarossa, *Unternehmen* 33, 59, 89, 137, 224, 237, 245
Brigadestab (brigade staff) 70
Bedford MWD light truck 241, 257
BMW R11 36
BMW R12 42
bridging equipment 227–31
Brigadestab (brigade staff) 70
Brückengerät 31, 43, 85, 219, 222–3, 225–6, 228
Bryansk 13
BT-7 23
Budapest 237
Büssing-NAG 56, 64, 194

Cruiser Tank A10 247
Cruiser Tank Mk 1 87
Czechoslovakia/Czech 46, 59–61, 71, 98, 189
Daimler-Benz 24, 50, 131
Daimler Dingo 247
de Gaulle, Colonel Charles 17
Divisionsjustizbeamter (divisional judicial officer) 79
Divisionsstab 70
Dunkirk 29, 54

Einheitsfahrgestell le Lkw 50

Fall Gelb (Plan Yellow) 70, 122
Fall Rot (Case Red) 8
Feldgendarmerie (field police) 240, 276–7
Feldküche (field kitchen) 80, 185, 222, 268, 270
Feldlazarett 236, 258–9
Feldpost (field post) 240, 274
FH 18 field howitzer 14, 55, 175–6, 181, 210, 212–13
FlaK 2cm 157, 206–9
FlaK 3.7cm 205
FlaK 8.8cm 209
FlaK 30, 2cm (SdKfz 10/4) 157, 204–5, 207, 237,
FlaK 38, 2cm (SdKfz 10/5) 157, 204, 206
Flakpanzer 203
Flammenwerfer 230
Flammpanzer 123, 217
Flers-Courcelette, battle of 7
Flugzeugabwehrkanone-Abteilungen (FlaKAbt) 127, 204
France 12, 15, 22, 29, 33–4, 39, 50, 54, 57, 61, 70–71, 80, 83, 85, 97, 121–2, 130, 147, 175, 199, 203, 222, 224, 226, 228, 242, 253, 256–7, 261, 277, 279
Fu 7 SE 20 U radio 66
Fu 8 SE 30 medium wave (MW) radio 66
Führungs-Abteilung (tactical group) 77
Funktrupp 62–4, 105, 108, 111, 132, 157

Great Britain 7, 29, 33, 50, 54, 63, 87, 241, 247, 257, 261, 279
Generalstab des Heeres (GenStbdH – General Staff of the Army) 21, 36
Generalstabsoffizier 77
Grenatwerfer (Gw – mortar) 159–61
großer Flosssäck 34 (large inflatable dinghy) 139, 219
große Kraftwagenkolonne (betriebsstoff) heavy transport column (fuel) 239, 241

Guderian, *Generaloberst* Heinz 13–15, 17, 21, 23, 41, 120, 121, 127, 130, 147, 229

Henschel 24, 50
Henschel *Typ* 33 D1 165, 242
Heye, *Generaloberst* August Wilhelm 13
high-explosive (HE) ammunition 23, 114, 141, 181, 183, 204, 235
Hilfswillige (Hiwis) 275
Hitler, Adolf 8–9, 21, 33, 43, 47, 75, 152, 237
Horch 48, 50, 55, 71, 119, 131, 176
Horch Kfz 12 249
Hoth, General Hermann 129
Hf 7 *Stahlfeldwagen* 242

Ju-52 transport 238, 261
Ju-87 Stuka 205
Kama 13, 21
Kfz 1 41, 47, 79, 90, 95, 99, 108, 111, 186
Kfz 2/40 79, 90, 95, 99, 108, 111, 254
Kfz 11 42, 47–8, 54, 79, 90, 99, 133, 138, 155, 159, 167, 179, 181, 267
Kfz 12 42, 47, 51, 95, 109, 111, 140, 157, 159, 176, 178–80, 181, 185, 191, 199, 249
Kfz 13 23
Kfz 15 63–4, 79, 90, 94–5, 99, 108–9, 111, 113, 132–3, 137, 139–41, 157–9, 166–8, 175–6, 178, 181, 185, 191, 194–5, 198, 204–5, 220–22, 266
Kfz 17 65–6, 111, 132–3, 141, 157–58, 166, 175–6, 185, 191, 194, 196
Kfz 21 41, 43, 47–8, 79, 90, 95, 108, 155
Kfz 23 *Fernsprechkraftwagen* (telephone car) 158, 176, 178
Kfz 31 79, 90, 95, 97, 99, 108, 111, 131, 140, 166, 221, 258, 260, 264–5
Kfz 69 48, 50, 54, 131, 139–41, 161, 168, 185
Kfz 305 260
Kraftfahrtruppen (motorized forces) 13–14

Kradschützen (motorcycle-mounted infantry) 29, 36, 107, 110, 130, 131, 137–8, 151, 159, 161, 167–70, 264

Kradschützen-Bataillon (KradSchtzBtl – motorcycle-mounted rifle battalion) 161

Kradschützen-Kompanie (KradSchtzKp – motorcycle rifle company) 137, 159, 167, 170

Krupp 24, 48, 50, 109

Kübelwagen 34, 37, 41, 45, 131

Kürbelmast 95, 197

KwK 37 136, 144

KwK L/24 7.5cm 114, 121, 132, 149

KwK 40 L/43 7.5cm 121, 152

KwK L/45 3.7cm 94, 122, 147

KwK L/60 5cm 123–4

Laffly W 15 T 39

Leichter Feldhaubitz (le FH – light field howitzer) 14, 27, 55, 175, 176, 210, 213

leichte Flugzeugabwehrkanone Abteilung (le FlaKAbt – light antiaircraft battalion) 125, 206

leichte Truppenluftschutzwagen (light anti-aircraft vehicles) 97

le Pkw 41, 47, 52, 79, 95, 99, 109, 111, 176, 222

Libya 87, 247

Low Countries 92

Luftwaffe 21, 29, 43, 66, 127, 160, 203, 238, 247

Lutz, *Generalmajor* Oswald 13–14, 23

Marita, *Unternehmen* 205

Marmon Herrington armoured car 136

Maybach 49, 71

Me 323 188

Mercedes-Benz L 1500A 46

Mercedes-Benz L 3000 159

Meuse, river 222

MG 34 28, 47, 51, 57, 60, 83, 97, 114, 121, 127, 137–8, 143, 159–61, 167, 169, 171

ML-20 216

Morris Commercial CS 8 29, 63

Nachrichtenzug (signals platoon) 90, 108, 157, 175, 178

Nachschub-Bataillon (supply battalion) 239

Nationalsozialistische Deutsche Arbeiterpartei (NSDAP – National Socialist German Workers' Party) 8

North Africa 37, 81, 83, 133, 136, 144, 189, 241, 272

Oberkommando der Wehrmacht (OKW – High Command of German Armed Forces) 22, 206

Opel *Blitz* (Lightning) *Typ* 2.5-35 54

Ordonnanzoffizier (special missions officer) 73

Organisations-Abteilung (OrgAbt – organization department) 33

PaK 3.7cm 29, 139, 141, 155, 161, 168, 171, 183–4, 187, 189, 221

PaK 38 5cm 189

PaK 40 7.5cm 56, 188

PaK 43 8.8cm 183, 203, 205, 215, 235

Panhard 178 – *Panzerspähwagen* 204(f) 129–30

Panzerjäger-Abteilung (PzJg-Abt – anti-tank battalion) 42

Panzernachrichten-Abteilung (armoured signals battalion) 79

Panzer-Pioniere (armoured engineers) 217

Panzerschreck-Raketenpanzerbüchse (RPzB) 101

Panzerschule (tank training school) 21

Panzerschürzen (side skirts) 121, 147, 149

Panzerspähwagen 22, 55–7, 127, 129–31, 137

Pionier-Zug (mot) (PiZug – engineer platoon [motorized]) 139

Poland 10, 12, 33–4, 57, 86, 122, 203, 217,

227, 114, 119, 237
PzBefWg III (SdKfz 267) 82, 91, 94–5, 97–8,
    220
PzGrenDiv Großdeutschland 82, 148, 152,
    170
PzKpfw 35(t) 59–61, 71, 152
PzKpfw 38(t) 15, 60–61, 152
PzKpfw I 8, 19, 25, 27, 34, 60–61, 72, 90,
    119, 147–9, 189, 222–3, 225, 229
PzKpfw II 8, 25, 28, 34, 60–61, 72, 85–6,
    90, 97, 101, 117, 119, 169, 147–9, 222–3,
    225–6
PzKpfw III 7–8, 23, 25, 28, 31, 60–61, 65,
    71–2, 94, 96, 98, 101, 114, 117–19, 122–5,
    147–9, 151–2, 201, 217, 227
PzKpfw IV 7–8, 15, 17, 23, 25, 28, 31, 60–61,
    65, 72, 77, 80, 114, 116–17, 119–21, 121,
    123, 125, 147, 147–9, 152, 173, 203,
    223–4, 228, 230, 254
PzKpfw V Panther 152, 223
PzKpfw VI Tiger 13, 152

Quartiermeister-Abteilung (quartermaster
    battalion) 77

Reichsbahn (German national railways) 239
Renault AH 199, 247
Renault Chenilette UE light tractor 195
Rommel, Erwin, General 15, 69, 81
Russia 33, 37, 94, 110, 130, 141–3, 151, 170,
    175, 189, 199, 211, 214–5, 229, 238–9,
    268, 276–7
Ryabinki 143, 211–13

Saurer RK 7 – SdKfz 254 (m gepBeobWg –
    medium armoured observation vehicle) 181
Scherenfernrohr (scissor-type periscope) 133,
    179
Schlächterei-Kompanie (mot) (butchery
    company [motorized]) 268

Schlachtkörper (combat corps) 123
Schützenpanzerwagen (SPw – armoured
    personnel carriers) 57, 80, 103, 124, 141–3,
    155, 166, 168, 224, 235
schwere Feldhaubitz (sFH – heavy field
    howitzer) 18 175–6, 215–7
schwere Kompanie (mot) (s Kp – heavy
    company [motorized]) 139, 142, 160, 167
schwere Panzerbüchse (s PzB – heavy anti-tank
    rifle) 235
Schwere Panzerspähwagen (PzSpWg) 57, 127,
    130, 135, 137
SdKfz Sonderkraftfahrzeug
  SdKfz 6 55, 181, 228
  SdKfz 7 55, 181, 205, 207, 212, 215, 220,
    256
  SdKfz 8 schwere Zugkraftwagen (s ZgKw –
    heavy half-track tractor) 155
  SdKfz 9 55, 115, 250
  SdKfz 10 185, 204–7, 221, 237, 257,
    268
  SdKfz 11 54, 155, 181
  SdKfz 106 204
  SdKfz 138 188
  SdKfz 221 55, 57, 97, 125, 133, 137
  SdKfz 222 17, 33, 55, 132, 137–8
  SdKfz 223 55, 136–7, 187, 251
  SdKfz 231 17, 56, 136–7, 163
  SdKfz 232 17, 22, 24, 56, 113, 135, 137
  SdKfz 234 56
  SdKfz 247 Ausf A 105
  SdKfz 247 Ausf B 48, 62, 105, 109, 113,
    133
  SdKfz 250 107, 132, 136, 138, 143, 151,
    155, 158, 160–1, 168, 170–1, 175
  SdKfz 250/9 138
  SdKfz 251 14, 80, 105, 116, 143, 155,
    159–63, 170, 183, 224, 234–5
  SdKfz 251/3 (m FuPzWg – medium
    armoured radio car) 79–80

SdKfz 251/8 (*Kanonenwagen*) 136
SdKfz 251/8, *mittlerer Krankenpanzerwagen* (m KrPzWg – medium armoured ambulance) 163, 234, 236–7
SdKfz 254 179
SdKfz 260 55, 127, 132, 141, 198–9
SdKfz 261 55, 63, 105, 110–111, 127, 132, 158–9, 166, 185, 194, 199
SdKfz 263 63–4, 70, 85, 104, 108, 132, 137, 187, 191, 194, 197–9
SdKfz 265 65–6, 78, 98, 152, 199
SdKfz 266 66–7, 97–8, 105
SdKfz 267 66, 69, 91, 94, 97–9, 191, 198
SdKfz 268 67, 94, 98, 198
Škoda 60
Sonderanhänger (SdAnh – special-purpose trailer) 41, 115, 140, 195, 199, 207, 252, 268–9
Soviet Union 13, 15, 21–3
Stab eines Schützen Battailons (rifle battalion staff) 108
Stalingrad 131, 261
Sterantenne (star antenna) 66, 73, 82
Sturmartillerie 253, 256

T-26 23
T-34 60, 211–12, 215
TornFu 133, 157–8, 166, 176, 178, 181, 185, 204, 221

Versailles, Treaty of 7, 9
von Seeckt, *Generaloberst* Johannes 'Hans' Friedrich Leopold 12–13
von Stülpnagel, *Generalleutnant* Otto 14
VW *Typ* 166 *Schwimmwagen* 107, 131

Zahlmeister (paymaster) 78
Zerstörungszug (demolition platoons) 222
Zitadelle, Unternehmen 123 (see Barbarossa)
Zugführerwagen (ZW – platoon commander

Acknowledgements

As with my previous books, I have used information found in several archives; primarily documents of German provenance stored in the Bundesarchiv/Militärarchiv, Freiburg, Germany and World War II files at the National Archives and Records Administrations, Washington, USA. A new player on this field is the internet-based 'Project for the Digitizing of German Documents in Archives of the Russian Federation', provided further precious documents.

The late Tom Jentz, must be remembered since he was the undisputed expert on history of German armoured vehicles. Also he was the founding editor of *Panzer Tracts*, the most authoritative publication on the subject and an excellent reference source.

My sincere thanks to Peter Müller of *Historyfacts*: A true friend, who not only provided rare photographs but also advice and assistance.

Also my gratitude to those who allowed me access to their photographic collection:

Florian von Aufseß

Joachim Baschin

Holger Erdmann

Daniele Guglielmi

Henry Hoppe

Peter Kocsis (PeKo Publishing)

Michael Kümmel

Karlheinz Münch

Jürgen Wilhelm

A number of contemporary images have been sourced from the archive of Süddeutsche Zeitung Photo of Munich (SZ Photo) and also Getty Images (Getty), in London.

Finally, my gratitude to my long-suffering editor, Jasper Spencer-Smith, whose skill and never-ending patience made this book possible.

Unless otherwise indicated, all images in this book are from the Thomas Anderson Collection.

Bibliography

Panzertruppen Volume 1 and Volume 2, Tom Jentz; Podzun-Pallas

Panzer Tracts, several volumes; Panzer Tracts, Boyds, MD, USA

British & American Tanks, Chamberlain/Ellis; J. F. Lehmanns Verlag

Die Panzertruppen, Heinz Guderian; Mittler & Sohn

Erinnerungen eines Soldaten, Heinz Guderian; Verlag Kurt Voswinkel

Kriegstagebuch, several volumes, General Halder Kohlhammer

Die deutschen Kampfwagen im Weltkriege, Major Volckheim; Mittler & Sohn

Tanks in the Patriotic War, Volume 1 and Volume 2, Soljankin etc; Eksprint, Moscow